The Dated Events of the Old Testament

Being a Presentation of
Old Testament Chronology

Eugene, Oregon

Wipf and Stock Publishers
199 W 8th Ave, Suite 3
Eugene, OR 97401

The Dated Events of the Old Testament
Being a Presentation of Old Testament Chronology
By Beecher, Willis J.
ISBN 13: 978-1-55635-220-11
ISBN 10: 1-55635-220-4
Publication date 1/24/2007
Previously published by Sunday School Times Company, 1907

DATED EVENTS OF THE
OLD TESTAMENT

PREFACE

The tables in this little volume present to the eye a reasonably complete list of the events narrated in the Old Testament, with their time relations: first of all the relations of each event to other near events, Israelitish or foreign, and also its date in terms of the Christian era. The tables distinguish between the dates which are fixed by positive evidence and those which are matters of conjectural opinion. They also present to the eye a conspectus of the evidence by which each event is dated, and the reasons for the variant opinions that men hold concerning the chronology. And not least important, they make graphic by means of their blank spaces the fact that in the Old Testament we have, never an attempt at a complete history, but everywhere narratives of selected incidents.

As to the structure and use of the tables see the Introduction, especially Chapter V.

CONTENTS

INTRODUCTION

CHAPTER I
The Chronological Data in the Old Testament

PAGE

Three kinds of numbers.—Time words.—Order of mention.—Nature of the events narrated 5

CHAPTER II
External Data for Old Testament Chronology

Jewish sources.—Greek and Roman sources.—Other ancient sources.—Compendiums of chronology.—Assyrian data.—Babylonian data.—Assyrio-Babylonian data.—Egyptian data.—Astronomical data.—Connecting links. 7

CHAPTER III
Chronological Units and Methods

The ancient year.—The two Jewish years.—The Old Testament year.—Does the Old Testament use different kinds of years?—Mode of counting time.—Tabulation the only method 11

CHAPTER IV
Limits and Value of Bible Chronology

The Ussher chronology.—Recent chronological schemes.—Biblical chronology compared with Assyrian.—Biblical chronology compared with Egyptian.—Egyptian minimum dates.—Biblical chronology compared with the earlier Assyrian and Babylonian.—Results of the comparisons 16

CHAPTER V
The Tables

General considerations.—Divisions of the history and the chronology.—The columns of numbers in the tables.—The explanatory columns.—How to use the tables.—"Accession-year" *versus* "first year."—The chronology of these tables compared with other chronologies.—Corollaries 28

TABLES OF OLD TESTAMENT CHRONOLOGY

FIRST TABLE

Dated events from Abraham to Joshua 35

SECOND TABLE

Introduction.—Dated events from Joshua to Solomon 77

CONTENTS

Third Table

	PAGE
Dated events from the disruption of the kingdom to the close of Old Testament history	125

Fourth Table

Introduction.—Dated events from the close of Old Testament history to the birth of Christ	177
Appendix	197
Index	199

INTRODUCTION

Chapter I

The Chronological Data in the Old Testament

Of the materials for chronology found in the Old Testament four kinds are perhaps of especial interest: the numerals, the time words, the order in which events are mentioned, the nature of the events.

1. *The Chronological Numbers.*—These are of three kinds: cardinal numbers, indicating the time an event lasted; ordinal numbers, indicating the date when an event occurred or began or ended; long numbers, measuring the interval between two distant events. For example (1 Ki. 15:33), Baasha began to reign the third year of Asa, and reigned twenty-four years. Here the cardinal number "twenty-four" states the duration of the event, and the ordinal number "third" dates its beginning. Examples of long numbers are the 480 of 1 Kings 6:1, the 300 of Judges 11:26, the 430 of Exodus 12:40.

2. *Time Words.*—Chronological facts are indicated by the use of certain connecting words and phrases, such as "afterward," "before this," indicating the order in which events occurred (*e. g.* Neh. 13:4 or 2 Sam. 8:1, 10:1, 6:1). One should look carefully to see whether the time phrase comes from the final narrator, or is part of a document quoted by him, for this might make an important difference. Such words as "then," in the English versions may not be time words, but may stand for the Hebrew "and," being used in English merely for the sake of variety.

3. *The Order in which a Narrative Mentions Events.*—This is commonly that in which they occurred. But sometimes, for various reasons, narrators speak of events in a different order from that in which they occurred. We need to have our eyes open for such variations in the order (see 4a below). Certain parts of the Old Testament history have been dreadfully muddled through neglecting facts of this kind.

4. *The Nature of the Events Narrated.*—This has obvious bearings on questions relating to the chronology.

    a. Sometimes we must infer the order of the events from their nature. For example, the narrative mentions the marriage of Ahab to Jezebel after its mention of his accession. But it also says that their grandson was 22 years old about 33 years after Ahab's accession, and this proves that the marriage occurred some years before the accession (1 Ki. 16:31; 2 Ki. 8:25–26). To bring up the ark from Kiriathjearim David gathered his officers and the Israelitish people from Shihor of Egypt to Hamath (1 Chron. 13:1–5), which shows that the event occurred relatively late in his reign, after he had conquered those regions, and not at its very beginning, as most readers have hastily supposed. If Phinehas, the grandson of Aaron, was living at the time of the civil war with Benjamin (Jud. 20: 28), then that event preceded most of the other events recorded in the book of Judges, and the chronology must be adjusted accordingly. Instances of this kind are so numerous and important that a due attention to them revolutionizes, at some crises in the history, the mechanical chronology which we have inherited from Josephus.

b. Again, events themselves occupy time. An event may be begun and finished within an hour, for example the slaying of Abner by Joab (2 Sam. 3: 27); or it may occupy the time of several human generations, for example the sojourn of Israel in Egypt. Or an event may belong to a certain period in a human life, and may in that way involve data of time. For example, the seduction of Dinah (Gen. 34) must have occurred after she had reached the age of adolescence, and after her brothers had become warriors grown; and this proves that it did not occur, as many have supposed, just thirteen years after her mother was first married. Since the accounts make the impression that Saul was an inexperienced young man when he became king, it follows that an interval of some years must have elapsed between the first acts of his reign (1 Sam. 11: 1–13: 2) and those recorded in the very next verses, in which his son Jonathan figures as a warrior of prowess. There are many similar cases. We may infer dates for events from the time required for human generations, or for the successive periods in a human life, or for a military campaign, or for a journey from one point to another, or for the recovery of the depleted population of a country, or for other events that require time.

c. Again, there are many important matters that depend on the nature of the events as belonging to some particular season of the year, or to some particular part of a month or week or day. To hide David's messengers the woman spread a covering over the well and strewed bruised corn upon it (2 Sam. 17: 19). The season was therefore that of freshly ripened grain, and attention to this will clear up several matters connected with the rebellion of Absalom. So in other instances.

d. Attention to the nature of the events also makes it possible to supplement the biblical data from without. When the Bible mentions Tiglath-pilezer or Cyrus or Darius, for example, if we know from other sources the dates of these men, that helps us to date the biblical events with which they were connected. And it is at least supposable that the Bible so mentions natural phenomena that we can apply astronomical or other computations for determining the dates at which they occurred.

Chapter II

External Data for Old Testament Chronology

External data are now much more abundant than they were in the times of Ussher and the other great biblical chronologists. To the Jewish and Greek and Latin sources which they possessed have now been added an immense body of facts accumulated in the explorations of the past sixty years.

5. *Jewish Sources.*—Certain extrabiblical Jewish sources of chronological information have long been known to scholars.

a. In the Septuagint and in the Samaritan copies of the Pentateuch are some numerals and other chronological data that differ from those in our Hebrew Bibles. The differences are especially important for the pre-Abrahamic times, but are not limited to these.

b. Josephus abounds in chronological data, in addition to those which he has copied from the Bible. His numerals have been carelessly copied, and it is evident that he had only very confused ideas of such matters as, for example, the succession of the kings of Persia. But he is generally reliable as a witness transmitting tradition, and in certain conditions his testimony to a number as traditional is of great importance.

c. The *Seder Olam* is a Jewish chronological work written early in the Christian era. The *Seder Olam Zutta* is an appendix to it, written many centuries later.

6. *Greek and Roman Sources.*—Herodotus, about B. C. 445, Diodorus Siculus, B. C. 44 nearly, Strabo, who died 25 A. D., with other classical writers, abound in chronological materials, more or less trustworthy, for the peoples with whom the Israelites came into contact.

7. *Other Ancient Sources.*—Certain ancient writers, Babylonian, Egyptian, Tyrian, etc., are cited by Josephus and the classical historians and their successors. Prominent among these are Berosus for the Babylonian history, and Manetho for the Egyptian. Accounts of them may be found in books of reference. Manetho wrote in Greek, at Alexandria, probably in the third century B. C. Fragments of his history of Egypt are preserved in Josephus (*Cont. Ap.* i, 14, 26 and contexts) and in Julius Africanus (see 8*b*). The fragments are often confused and contradictory, but they are still an important source for Egyptian chronology.

8. *Compendiums of Chronology.*—There were ancient attempts to arrange history in chronological schemes, some of which have relations with the chronology of the Bible.

a. The introduction of eras began early. We are familiar with the Roman methods of dating by consulships, or from the founding of the city; and with the Greek methods by olympiads, or by the terms of the Archons. Among usages of this sort the so-called Seleucid era is especially connected with the biblical chronology, being that so often mentioned in the books of the Maccabees and in Josephus as "the year of the Greeks." It was initiated by the Seleucid Greek dynasty at Antioch, its first year corresponding to B. C. 312.

b. Lists of dated historical events have been known from ancient times. To say nothing of the work of Manetho and Berosus and others (mentioned in 7), a famous book of this kind is the *Chronographia* of Julius Africanus, written about 220 A. D., and now extant only in the fragments quoted by Eusebius in his *Chronicon*, written about 325 A. D., and in the citations made, in part from the *Chronicon* and in part from a copy of Africanus, by the monk Georgius Syncellus of the ninth century.

c. On the whole the most important of these compendiums is the one which is commonly described as the Canon of Ptolemy, made by Claudius Ptolemæus, an Alexandrian geographer and astronomer and mathematician, in the second century after Christ. In the form in which it is available for our use it is a list of sovereigns, Babylonian, Persian, Greek, Egyptian, and Roman, beginning B. C. 747, and extending to the time of the author. By its aid the date of any astronomical or other occurrence of that period can be stated as in such and such a year of such and such a king. In the Ussher chronology this canon is undervalued, but it is now regarded as accurate. At certain points Ptolemy may have been mistaken as to his political facts, but not so as to affect his presentation of the succession of the years.

9. *Additional Sources Uncovered by Modern Explorations.*—These are numerous and valuable, both for enabling us to understand the data that were previously known, and as furnishing additional data. We can here look only at some of the more important.

10. *Assyrian Data.*—*a.* The most important single document is the one which, following Mr. George Smith, we will call the Assyrian Eponym Canon. Other Assyriologists give various other designations to it. For certain purposes the Assyrians named the year after a certain public official; and the canon is a list of these officers, one for each year. No complete copy is known, but by piecing together what remains of several different copies there is a continuous list of about 265 names, up to B. C. 647, with a broken list for the decades later than that. So the list covers the time from soon after the close of Solomon's reign to the reign of Josiah. Some copies have historical notes appended, and these are generally, though not always, confirmed by the other Assyrian data. It is possible that some of the existing copies were made as early as the seventh century before Christ, before the downfall of Assyria. There are some slight discrepancies, but the list is in a high degree trustworthy.

b. There are also now available many records of Assyrian kings. For example, we have annals of Shalmanezer II, Tiglath-pilezer III, Sargon, Sennacherib, Esarhaddon, Asshurbanipal, giving dated accounts of their exploits, year by year, besides other accounts which mention occasional dates. Long numbers are also given. For example, Sennacherib says that he brought back certain gods which had been taken to Babylon 418 years previously, in the time of Tiglath-pilezer. In some of these records a king mentions another as his son, or mentions his father or grandfather, thus marking the reigns as continuous. These records variously supplement and interpret the canon.

    c. In addition there have been discovered records of temples, votive tablets, laws, records of business transactions, including dated events that serve to fill out those in the important documents.

    d. The Assyrian chronology has two methods of designating any given year. The year which we designate B. C. 678 is in the canon of Ptolemy the third year of Esarhaddon, king of Babylon (and Assyria). The Assyrians would sometimes designate it in the same way, the third year of Esarhaddon. But they would also designate it as the year of the eponymy of Nergal-sar-utsur, and the following year as that of Abramu, and so forth.

    11. *Babylonian Data.*—No Babylonian eponym list is known. But there are Babylonian documents, especially what may in a general way be called the Babylonian chronicles, written in the Persian period or earlier, including lists of dynasties, lists of kings with the number of years they reigned, and other lists with dated records of exploits in the reign of each king. The data also include long numbers, especially summaries of the duration of the successive dynasties. Add to these the same kinds of private documents as are found among the Assyrian sources.

    12. *Assyrio-Babylonian Data.*—From very early times the history of Assyria and that of Babylonia were interwoven, and there are some chronological materials that are common to the two.

    a. There are fragments of writings that gave a synchronous history of the two countries. They describe the relations and the exploits of Babylonian and Assyrian kings who were contemporaries, frequently dating events by year, month, and day. Some of them carry the chronology far back, but they exist in so mutilated a form that they do not give us a continuous chronology.

    b. Some of the long numbers compare Babylonian events with Assyrian.

    13. *Egyptian Data.*—These are abundant and various, but they give us no continuous scheme of dates. All alleged continuous schemes are inferential. That none of them are final may be inferred from the fact that they are numerous, and increasing in number. The older sources give us three different and disagreeing recensions of the numbers of Manetho. The newer sources include tables giving lists of kings, and superabundant materials for some parts of the history, including portraits of kings and distinguished men, their authentic mummies, memoranda of their exploits and their business transactions and their religious worship and their home life and their ideas. In these materials are immense numbers of dates. At points in the history we are able to date minutely fragmentary successions of events. But anything like a complete Egyptian chronology is still out of reach.

    14. *Astronomical Data.*—Ancient records sometimes mention astronomical

phenomena that are capable of being identified, and of being verified by calculation. A particularly important instance of this kind is an eclipse of the sun mentioned in the Assyrian records as occurring in the tenth year of Asshur-daan III, the calculated date of which is June 15, B. C. 763.

Correct astronomical calculations are in themselves decisive, but the identification of the phenomena on which they are based is often merely conjectural. Most attempts to connect them with biblical dates are insufficiently grounded. Men connect them with many Egyptian facts of different kinds, but no consensus has been reached.

15. *Connecting Links between the Biblical and the Ethnical Chronologies.*— With Assyria and Babylonia these are numerous and exact, and the continuity with modern chronology is complete. For instance, the first year of Nebuchadrezzar of Babylon was the year that began in March, B. C. 604. This was the fourth year of Jehoiakim, king of Judah (Jer. 25:1, etc.). From such coincidences one may derive a complete scheme of dates. The Egyptian connections are less certain and less exact.

Chapter III

Chronological Units and Methods

16. *The Ancient Year.*—*a.* Our month-names, September, October, November, December, the Latin for seventh month, eighth month, etc., are a monument of the fact that the year of the ancient world was prevailingly that which began at a new moon near the spring equinox. Whether determined astronomically, or by watching the crops, or by noting the point of time when the days and nights were of equal length, or in some other way, this "vernal" year, fixed by natural phenomena of some kind, and not by a mere count of months and days, was very widely recognized. We may conveniently describe it as "the year that began in March," and this is accurate enough for most purposes. This was the current year of the Babylonians and Assyrians, and is, as we shall see, the year commonly used in the Bible.

b. Far back in history can be traced the recognition of other years than this. It is commonly said that the Seleucid year (see 8a) began in September. The Egyptians had two or more kinds of years (see 24). But the year beginning with a new moon near the spring equinox is of principal importance in ancient chronology, and for most purposes no other year need be considered.

17. *The Two Jewish Years.*—We are familiar with the fact that the Jews of our time celebrate their new year in September, and that two Jewish years are recognized, commonly called the sacred and the secular. The following is the order of the months in these years.

Sacred.	Secular.		Sacred.	Secular.	
1	7	Abib, or Nisan.	7	1	Tizri.
2	8	Iyyar, or Ziv.	8	2	Bul.
3	9	Sivan.	9	3	Chislev.
4	10	Thammuz.	10	4	Tebeth.
5	11	Ab.	11	5	Shebat.
6	12	Elul.	12	6	Adar.

To the sacred year might be added the intercalary thirteenth month called W'adar, "And-Adar."

18. *The Old Testament Year.*—Old Testament chronology has been greatly muddled, from the time of Josephus, by the assumption that it counts secular events in autumnal years. In fact it uses the vernal year so uniformly that no account need be taken of any other.

a. The accounts of the exodus recognize only the year that has Abib for its first month (*e. g.* Ex. 13:4, 12:2, 23:15, 34:18), the passover being in Abib, which is declared to be the first month, and is identified by its relations to the harvest. In these passages the autumnal feast is said to be at the "going out of the year" (Ex. 23:16), the "coming around of the year" (Ex. 34:22; cf. 2 Chron. 24:23; 1 Sam. 1:20; Ps. 19:6, these being all the places where the word is used),

The parallel phrase "the turning back of the year" appears five times (2 Sam. 11:1; 1 Chron. 20:1; 1 Ki. 20:22, 26; 2 Chron. 36:10). In themselves these phrases might easily be understood to indicate the termination of one year, which is the beginning of another, and so as indicating an autumnal year. In fact, however, their contexts show that the conception intended is that of the middle of the year, the goal from which the year "turns back," retraces its steps to the point where it began; from which it "comes around" to its starting point; where it completes its "going out" and begins its coming in. At its start the days and nights were of equal length. On its march the days have been longer than the nights, but at the turning point they become equal again. On the return march the nights are longer than the days, but they become equal when the vernal equinox is reached again.

The details of the three yearly feasts presuppose the conception of the vernal year (e. g. Lev. 23: 5–36). In Joshua (e. g. 4: 19, 5: 10, 11) we are told that Israel crossed the Jordan the first month, which is identified as the passover month. Dozens of passages might be cited.

b. The passages cited and many others affirm that the year having Nisan for the first month was appointed by Jehovah through Moses. From Josephus (*Ant.* I, iii, 3) down men have inferred that the vernal year was then a new institution, introduced by Moses. But the accounts do not say this, and it is in itself improbable. Apparently it was the Babylonian year, brought thence by Abraham at his migration. In Egypt Israel may have reckoned by Egyptian years as well as Babylonian, but now declared itself independent of the Egyptian usage.

c. That this year beginning near the spring equinox was the sacred year of Israel is affirmed in the passages cited and in many others (e. g. Lev. 16: 29, 23: 5, 24, 27; Num. 9: 1, 5, 11, 28: 16, 29: 1, 7; 2 Chron. 5: 3, 7: 10; Ezra 6: 19; Neh. 7: 73–9: 1; 1 Ki. 12: 32, 33), and is disputed by no one.

d. This same vernal year is used in reckoning secular affairs. The ninth month (Jer. 36: 22, 23) when Jehoiakim burned Baruch's roll was at the season when fire was used for warmth. Therefore it was not the summer month Sivan, the ninth month of the autumnal year, but the winter month Chislev, the ninth month of the vernal year. The seventh month (Jer. 40, 41, especially 40: 10, 41: 8, 1; 2 Ki. 25: 25) when men in the hill country of Judah had stored up corn and wine and oil and fruits from the deserted farms was not Nisan, the seventh month of the autumnal year, but Tizri, the seventh month of the vernal year. The successive dated events of the exodus are expressed in terms of the year that began in the month when Israel left Egypt, that is, the month of the spring equinox. They started from their houses the fifteenth day of the first month, from Elim the fifteenth of the second month, reached the wilderness of Sinai the third month, set up the tent of meeting the first day of the second year, "declared their pedigrees" the first day of the second month, started from Sinai the twentieth day of that month, received the returning spies in the time of grapes and pomegranates and figs, gathered again at Kadesh the first month of the fortieth year conquered Sihon and Og several months later, were on the east bank of the Jordan the first day of the eleventh month, mourned thirty days for Moses, crossed the river early the first month of the following year (Ex. 12: 18, 29–37, 16: 1, 19: 1, 40: 2, 17; Num. 1: 18, 10: 11, 13: 20, 23, 20: 1, 21: 21ff; Deut. 1: 3, 34: 8; Josh. 4: 19).

e. In particular, we find it used in counting the regnal years of kings. The first month of the first year of Hezekiah, as counted in Chronicles, was the passover month (2 Chron. 29: 3, 17, cf. 30: 1–3, 13, 15). The same year, the months of the harvest of corn and wine and oil in the uplands were from the third to the seventh (2 Chron. 31: 7). The second month of the fourth year of Solomon's reign was Ziv, and the eighth month of his eleventh year was Bul (1 Ki. 6: 1, 37, 38; cf. 2 Chron. 3: 2). The first month of the twelfth year of Ahasuerus is Nisan, the twelfth is Adar, the third is Sivan, the tenth month of the seventh year is Tebeth (Esth. 3: 7, 12, 13, 8: 9, 2: 16). The ninth month of the fourth year of Darius was Chislev, and the eleventh month of his second year was Shebat (Zech. 7: 1, 1: 7; cf. the dates in Haggai).

f. Is there proof that any other way of reckoning years was customary in Israel in Old Testament times? There is a traditional interpretation to this effect, but is it well grounded?

The flood of Noah began in the second month, the ark rested the seventh month, the mountain-tops were seen the tenth month, the earth was generally visible the first month of the following year, and was dry the latter part of the second month (Gen. 7: 11, 8: 4, 5, 13, 14). Josephus says (*Ant.* I, iii, 3) that this second month was Bul, the second month of the autumnal year. Sayce says (*Early Hist. of the Hebrews*, p. 126) that this was the second month of the autumnal year, the beginning of the rainy season, the "seventh month" being the time when the early rains are over. I do not care to controvert this view, though the proof of it is not perfect.

The translation "the end of the year" (Ex. 23: 16, 34: 22) has misled English readers into thinking that the autumnal feast was at the close of one year and the beginning of another. See *a* above.

The fact that a law was made appointing the year that begins with Abib (Ex. 12: 2) may justify the inference that the Israelites knew of more ways than one of counting the year, so that the matter needed regulating, but nothing further than that. See *b* above.

The blowing of trumpets in the seventh month (Lev. 25: 4, 9) is perpetuated in the new year festivities now practiced by the Jews, but there is no proof that it was anciently regarded as marking the beginning of a calendar year.

Jeremiah's phrase "unto the completing of the eleventh year of Zedekiah * * *, unto the going of Jerusalem into exile in the fifth month" (Jer. 1: 3) has been cited as indicating a year that closed with the fifth month. But this interpretation is not according to biblical usage. See 19.

In Nehemiah mention is made of the month Chislev in the twentieth year of Artaxerxes, followed by the mention of Nisan in his twentieth year (1: 1, 2: 1). Perhaps, though not necessarily, the autumnal year is here intended, Chislev being the third and Nisan the seventh month.

However you decide these instances, there is not one of them that affects the chronology. And there is no important Old Testament instance in which we need to take into the account any other year than the one beginning near the spring equinox.

19. *Mode of Counting Time, in the Bible.*—Four closely related peculiarities should be noticed. First, the Bible writers count time by units only, disregarding fractions. Second, broken terminal units are for this reason liable to an ambiguous interpretation. Third, so are ordinal numbers. Fourth, the final unit of a series is sometimes used without regard to the initial unit.

a. They reckon by units only. The three days that our Saviour lay in the grave (in Matt. 12: 40 "three days and nights") were not three times twenty-four hours, but were part of Friday, the whole of Saturday, and part of Sunday, not much more than 36 hours in all. It was a period of time which included either wholly or in part three consecutive units of 24 hours each. Let this serve as a typical instance of the difference between our usual way of reckoning and the biblical way. In the biblical way years or days are not thought of as properly measures of time, but as current periods wholly or partly covered by the events spoken of. We use a like method in such matters as postage or mileage. A letter requires one stamp for each ounce or fraction of an ounce. The fraction is counted as if it were a full ounce.

b. They count a fraction of a terminal unit as if it were a complete unit. The calendar year during which a king dies and is succeeded by another is counted as the last year of the outgoing king. The whole of it is counted to him. It is not divided, as we should divide it. In the Assyrian records, the year is also counted to the incoming king, not as his first year, however, but as his accession year, his first year being the one that begins with the following new year. For example, Nebuchadrezzar became king at some time during the year that began in March, B. C. 605, but that year is counted as the twenty-first year of his father Nabopolassar, while the first year of Nebuchadrezzar was the year that began in the following March. He was actually king for several months before his "first year" began.

In the Bible the broken year at the close of a reign is always counted to the outgoing king, but it is sometimes also counted to the incoming king, being in these instances counted twice.

c. From this may arise an ambiguity in the use of ordinal numbers. When it is said that a king began to reign in a certain year of another king, the meaning may be that his first year is coincident with the designated year of the other king, or it may be that his accession occurred during that year, so that the coincidence is with his accession year, and not with his first year. For instances see the numbers, as given in the following tables, for the kings of Israel and of Judah just after the disruption.

d. Another form of this habit of counting by units and disregarding fractional parts appears in certain cases in which time is counted to a final terminus only, neglecting the initial terminus. Samson's wife is said to have wept "the seven days that their feast lasted," though she did not begin the weeping earlier than the fourth of those days (Jud. 14: 17, 14). In this way of speaking the seven days or other longer period is conceived of as if it were a unit, like a year or a day. An event completed in the last year or day of such a period is spoken of as if it had covered the period, irrespective of the time when it actually began. The Israelites are said to have wandered 40 years in the wilderness, though the wandering did not begin till the second year of the forty. The 400 years that Israel was to sojourn in Egypt may supposably count from the time when the matter was revealed to Abraham, and the 430 years of the sojourn from the time when Abraham came to Canaan. As we shall see, the formula in Judges, "And the land was quiet 40 years," in each case means that the land was quiet until the close of the forty-year period then current, the quiet in some cases being only during the few last years of the period (Num. 14: 33; Gen. 15: 13; Ex. 12: 40; Jud. 3: 11, 30, 5: 31, 8: 28).

20. *Tabulation the Only Feasible Method.*—We have found that the Bible states numerical facts in ways different from those to which we are accustomed, and that some of its statements may have more than one interpretation. This does not necessarily render its statements uncertain or difficult to understand. The true meaning is seldom in doubt provided we pursue a correct method. But the question of method is exceedingly important.

For example, the numbers given for the years of the kings of Israel from Jeroboam to Joram are 22 plus 2 plus 24 plus 2 plus 12 plus 22 plus 2 plus 12, a total of 98. The numbers for Judah for the same period are 17 plus 3 plus 41 plus 25 plus 8 plus 1, a total of 95. This is often cited by superficial reasoners as an instance of contradiction, discrediting the numbers. It is as if you handed your clerk two bundles of letters to mail, each bundle weighing a pound, but the two made up of letters of unlike weights, and then accused him of cheating you because he used twenty stamps for one pound and twenty-four for the other. Or it is as if you should expect two agents, traveling with mileage books from Chicago to New York, to use the same amount of mileage, though one stopped at way stations, and the other at express stations only.

Many of the problems in Bible chronology cannot be solved by processes of mere addition and subtraction or averaging or conjectural correction. Attempts of that kind are blunders. The only solution is by studying each particular number and ascertaining how it is used. This is not difficult provided one has patience and some feasible way of expressing his results by tabulation. There is no solution except by some process which shall make the numbers check and interpret each other. Using such a process one will find that there are no contradictions in the numbers above cited, and that the total of the years is neither 98 nor 95, but just 90, the differences being accounted for by co-reigns or by the counting of the terminal years to more kings than one.

Chapter IV

Limits and Value of Bible Chronology

21. *The Ussher Chronology.*—This system, found in the margins of many Bibles, is at most points admirably accurate. Its greatest fault is its attempt to reduce the history to millennial periods. Ussher believed that the earth was created just 4000 years before the birth of Jesus, and that Solomon's temple was dedicated just 1000 years before the birth of Jesus, and he pulls some parts of the chronology awry, to make it fit this theory. He regards the biblical numbers for the times before Abraham as chronological, which I think is a mistake. He adopts the mistaken method of trying to adjust years by fractional parts, after our modern fashion, instead of recognizing the custom of counting the fraction as a unit; but this does not often cause important differences. There are some matters of detail in which he lacked information which is now accessible.

22. *Recent Chronological Schemes.*—There are other old theories besides that of Ussher, but we need not delay with them. During the past half century a multitude of new theories have appeared. They are as various as the men who make them, but many of them are open to the following criticisms.

a. They use fallacious methods of reasoning. For example, they reject testimony with a thoroughly unscientific lack of discrimination. In particular, they neglect alike the biblical numerals and the biblical statements of fact. Some of them adopt the process of computing minimum dates, and afterward treating these as if they were average or even established dates. Almost of necessity this results in grave error. Further, the habit is common of relying upon astronomical computations and other exact processes, even when these are connected with the events only by slight conjectures. Further still, there is the habit of disposing of difficulties by resorting to averages or to conjectural corrections. Illustrations of these various mistaken methods will presently be given. Any of these processes may have a certain genuine value, but none of them give facts. If we cannot get at the facts without them, then the only thing to do is to confess that we do not know the facts.

b. Perhaps the worst of all the schemes of this kind are the compromise chronologies which have appeared in some Teachers' Bibles and in other helps to Bible study. A date in the terms of the Ussher chronology, whether correct or incorrect, is at least a definite date. A date in the terms of a scheme which cuts out a section from the Ussher chronology for the times of the judges, and another for the times after Solomon, may supposably be a definite date. But a date that is based on a compromise between the two has nothing to recommend it. Unfortunately, a good deal of compromise dating has found its way into our literature on the Bible.

23. *Bible Chronology as Compared with That of Assyria and Babylonia.*—So

far as the matter can be traced they are in very exact agreement, except in one exceedingly important matter.

a. The reign of Asshur-daan III of Assyria was contemporary with the latter part of that of Uzziah of Judah. The first year of Asshur-daan was the year that began in March of B. C. 772. In June of his tenth year occurred an eclipse, which astronomical computation has fixed as in June of B. C. 763. Back to these dates the cord of continuous chronology has from eight to a dozen firm strands, and is unbreakable.

One strand is the Assyrian eponym canon, covering this period from about B. C. 640 backward. A second strand is the fact that the Assyrian kings are in many cases expressly said to be either father and son, or otherwise in immediate succession. A third strand is the fact that of several of these kings we have annals mentioning their exploits year by year. A fourth strand is supplied for parts of the period in other dated Assyrian events. A fifth strand is Ptolemy's canon of Babylonian kings, back to B. C. 747. A sixth is found in the synchronous histories of Babylonia and Assyria, verifying many particular points in the line. A seventh (though imperfect) strand consists of other dated Babylonian or Egyptian events. An eighth strand is the long numbers given by Sennacherib and Nabonidus and others. A ninth is the biblical chronological numbers. A tenth is the biblical events interpreting and confirming the numbers. An eleventh is the long numbers of the Bible and Josephus. A twelfth is the astronomical calculation of the eclipse of Asshur-daan. Others might be specified in addition.

b. In the earlier period covering the time from Asa, king of Judah, to the earlier years of Uzziah's predecessor, Amaziah, there are synchronisms just as exact, though the cord has fewer strands. The Assyrian canon covers this period. There are several Assyrian kings who claim to be father and son, or otherwise in immediate succession. Some of them have left annals, celebrating their exploits year by year. We know of other events in their reigns less systematically dated. There are Babylonian synchronisms. And in the middle of this period Shalmanezer II claims that in his sixth year he defeated Benhadad and Ahab, and that in his eighteenth year he received tribute from Jehu. A reference to the table will show that the sixth year of Shalmanezer was the twenty-first of Ahab, and his eighteenth year the accession year of Jehu, and that it is impossible to move the synchronism even one year forward or backward.

c. For these periods the different lines of testimony, Assyrian, Babylonian, Ptolemaic, biblical, are sometimes spoken of as agreeing in a general way, so that they mainly confirm one another. A reference to the details in the tables will show that the synchronisms are exact, and not merely general, provided we count in vernal years, and otherwise follow the principles of interpretation laid down in the last chapter; and will further show that variant facts, difficult of explanation, are exceedingly rare.

Men have not been slow to infer from this the correctness of the Assyrian chronology. Certainly it is correct, being confirmed by a multitude of facts, and by the Ptolemaic and biblical chronologies, and by astronomical calculation. This condition of things is equally a confirmation of the correctness of Ptolemy's canon. But we should not neglect the fact that *it is also equally a confirmation of the correctness of the biblical data.* Strange to say, this has been overlooked. At these lines of contact the biblical chronology stands on the same footing of established correctness with the others.

d. Different is the period between the two Assyrian kings Ramman-nirari III and Asshur-daan III, from the middle of the reign of Amaziah to the latter part of the reign of Uzziah. For this interval the Assyrian canon has only the 10 years of the reign of Shalmanezer III, while the biblical data seem to call for 61 years. How shall we deal with this apparent contradiction?

At this point the number of strands in the cord is a minimum. There is no Ptolemaic canon, no statement as to Shalmanezer's relations to the kings who preceded or followed him, no annals giving the yearly exploits of kings, no synchronous history of Babylonia and Assyria, no other significant extrabiblical events, no astronomical computation. Of the remaining lines of evidence some are on one side and some on the other. On the side of the shorter chronology there is simply the list of names which constitute the canon, confirmed by certain long numbers[1] which show that some later Assyrian and Babylonian chronologers regard this list as continuous. For this chronology just these two strands here remain; all the others have vanished. In favor of the longer chronology are the biblical numbers, confirmed by the biblical accounts of the events, and by the long numbers found in the Bible and in Josephus (see the tables). To these three strands another of great strength is added when we find from the Egyptian data that the invasion of Shishak in Rehoboam's time (1 Ki. 14:25) cannot have been as late as B. C. 927, the Assyrian date for it, but was probably at the time indicated by the biblical date, B. C. 978 (see 25*a*).

The two views thus indicated are discrepant by 51 years. How shall we dispose of the discrepancy? There are probably but three alternatives that need to be considered. Either the Assyrian state writers omitted a period of 51 years, perhaps because the events were discreditable to Assyria; or the biblical and Egyptian numbers overlap one another, and can in some way be reduced so as to agree with the Assyrian; or the biblical accounts are to be rejected as untrustworthy.

The third of these alternatives is at present fashionable, but clearly it ought not to be accepted without reason. Several creditable attempts have been made

---

[1] For example, a tablet of Sennacherib quotes a tablet of Ramman-nirari as having been buried and found again after 101 years (Smith's *Assyr. Canon*, pp. 77, 205). In Sennacherib's Bavian inscription, lines 48-50 (*Rec. of Past*, IX, 21), he speaks of bringing back the gods that had been in Babylon 418 years, from the time of Marduk-nadin-ahhi, king of Akkad, and Tiglath-pilezer, king of Assyria. There are also instances of the time of the Babylonian king Nabonidus, going back to periods much earlier (*Rec. of Past*, III and IV, new series). Such data seem to prove that the later Assyrian scribes held the eponym list, as we have it, to be continuous (see instance in 26).

to work out the second, so far as the biblical data are concerned.[1] But the first should also be considered. Some say that the Assyrian eponym list is so well accredited in its other parts that we are unreasonable if we doubt this part of it. But, as we have already seen, the Bible numbers that here contradict it are exactly as well accredited, and by the same pieces of evidence. As the canon is merely a list of names, nothing could be easier than that 51 names might fall out of it, either by design or by accident. This would be the easier because the number of copies can never have been large, and the list was in the control of the state scribes. If they dropped certain names, their successors would of course follow the list as thus transmitted, and all trace of the omitted names would disappear in two or three generations. The time in question is that of the generations immediately preceding Tiglath-pilezer III, who was king of both Assyria and Babylon. It is a fact that those times were disastrous to Assyria, and that the history we have of them is obscure. It is also a fact that the traditions concerning the canon of Ptolemy affirm that the chronological records were tampered with for the times before Nabonassar, the contemporary of Tiglath-pilezer, and assign this as the reason why Ptolemy did not carry back his list further. Additional evidence may come to light, but as the case stands there is no reason why one should surrender the biblical dates in favor of the Assyrian.

e. Back to the downfall of Samaria in B. C. 718, the chronological differences only concern the ways of interpreting particular instances. For the time of the reign of Ramman-nirari III and earlier, the biblical dates may be transposed into the Assyrian by subtracting 51. For the intermediate dates the problem is not so simple. When you crowd the events of a hundred years into fifty years, that misplaces the events, and renders the dates uncertain.

24. *Bible Chronology as Compared with Egyptian.*—Modern Egyptologists make much of astronomical data. Each advocate of a scheme regards his scheme as having the certainty of a mathematical calculation. But there are many schemes, and they disagree by centuries. Each chain has links of the solid steel of astronomical computation, but they are tied together in places with rotten twine of conjecture.

In these schemes the Sothic cycle figures largely. The Egyptians reckoned time by a year of 365 days, while an astronomical year is $365\frac{1}{4}$ days nearly. Every four years the beginning of their common year of 365 days came one day earlier in the season, and so in the course of time it wandered through all the seasons. Hence, this year is called the wandering or vague year. If the day when the star Sothis first became visible before sunrise was the first day of one vague year, it would be the second day of the vague year four years later, and so on. If some stage of the overflow of the Nile occupied the third month of a vague year, it would, a hundred and twenty years later, occupy the fourth month. So with all the other phenomena of the seasons. As 1461 vague years equal 1460 astronom-

---

[1] See, for example, the article on "Chronology" in the Bible Dictionary of Dr. John D. Davis, or the article by the Rev. L. P. Badger in the *Old Testament Student* for June, 1886.

ical years nearly, these numbers indicate the length of a complete cycle of changes. Concerning the cycle itself there is no room for doubt. But it may be open to question whether the Egyptian reckoning by vague years always remained uninterrupted and uniform; and there is room for dispute as to the points of connection between the cycle and the events of the history.

Two of these schemes especially require mention.

a. The first is that of Lepsius, generally accepted a few years ago by scholars who disregarded the biblical data, including many who would object to being so classed. A Sothic cycle known as that of Menōphres terminated in 139 A. D. (others say within the four years that began in July, 140 A. D), and therefore began B. C. 1322. The identification of this Menōphres is conjectural. But if he was a king of Egypt, and if the name, being misspelled, is one more variant for Merneptah, and if this particular Merneptah was the Amenôphis to whose reign Manetho and Josephus assign the exodus, and if they are correct in so assigning it, then the exodus occurred about B. C. 1320. Other considerations were urged, and the evidence was affirmed to be cumulative, and the biblical numbers inconsistent with it were discarded. If we separate the Egyptian events from the biblical, Lepsius held that the year B. C. 1322 was connected with the reign of Merneptah, the immediate successor of Rameses II. Confidently as this theory was held, it is now abandoned, though some unwittingly still give dates based upon it.

b. Its former adherents now commonly accept the theory presented by Mahler, Edouard Meyer and others. An admirable account of this theory may be found in Professor Breasted's *Ancient Records*, I, 23–48. It is based on the Sothic cycle, with the claim that points of contact with the history have now actually been established, and that the important dates have therefore been fixed within narrow limits of possible variation.

Its advocates differ, however, notwithstanding their claim of being exact. The year in which Merneptah succeeded Rameses II is fixed by Petrie as B. C. 1207, by Sayce as B. C. 1280, by Breasted as B. C. 1225. The synchronism of Amenôphis IV of Egypt with Burna-buriash of Babylon and Asshur-uballit of Assyria, who are said by some to have flourished about B. C. 1430, formerly used in confirmation of the Lepsian dates, is now used in confirmation of these other dates, which differ from the Lepsian by from 40 to 120 years!

On this scheme the reign of Thutmose III of the eighteenth Egyptian dynasty is astronomically fixed as beginning May 3, B. C. 1501 (*Anc. Rec.* I, 31), and various other events are dated with the same exactness. We shall presently see that this is in contradiction with accepted historical facts, and that the alleged basis for astronomical calculations is wrongly placed, so that the whole scheme needs readjustment.

25. *Egyptian Minimum Dates.*—Certain facts concerning Egypt, gradually accumulated during the past few decades, are of great value for testing the schemes that have been presented. On the monuments are mentioned dated events of the reigns of many of the kings. By collating these we may obtain a minimum

number for the years of a period. If the ninth year of a king is mentioned on the monuments, that shows that he reigned at least those nine years, though it does not show how many more years he reigned. Working on this basis, we have some very solid facts, provided we use them correctly. Of especial importance is their bearing on the questions concerning Sheshonk I. (Shishak), the first king of the Egyptian twenty-second dynasty, and concerning the eighteenth and nineteenth dynasties.

a. Shishak was contemporary with Solomon (1 Ki. 11:40), and invaded Judah the fifth year of Rehoboam (1 Ki. 14:25). According to the Egyptian records this invasion was not later than the twentieth year of Shishak. The biblical numbers place it in B. C. 978, and the Assyrian in B. C. 927. Which date do the Egyptian records support?

According to the Assyrian records, supported by the biblical, Shabaka, the So of the Bible, the first king of the twenty-fifth Egyptian dynasty, was on the throne when Sargon invaded Palestine in B. C. 720. How long he had then reigned we are not told. Call the date of his accession B. C. 720 plus x. Add to it the minimum years for the preceding kings back to Shishak, and we shall have a minimum date for Shishak. In doing this we will use Professor Breasted's numbers for the minimum years.

Accession of Shabaka............	B. C. 720 plus	x
Twenty-fourth dynasty, years.........	6	
Twenty-third dynasty............	37 plus	$3x$
Twenty-second dynasty............	230 plus	$6x$
Accession of Shishak............	B. C. 993 plus	$10x$

We have the data for a variant form of this computation. Tirhakah, the second king after Shabaka, was on the throne (2 Ki. 19:9) at the time of Sennacherib's invasion, B. C. 701.

Accession of Tirhakah............	B. C. 701 plus	x
Previous kings of the dynasty, years..	24	
Accession of Shabaka............	B. C. 725 plus	x
Accession of Shishak............	B. C. 998 plus	$10x$

This expression for the date of Shishak has the same value with the other, the five years added to the numeral being taken from the x.

To get the true date we must augment the 998 by the value of the $10x$, and must diminish it by the amount of another unknown quantity, namely the number of the years that are counted twice by reason of overlapping reigns. Professor Breasted estimates the latter at 30 years, and we provisionally accept his estimate. But what is the numerical value of the $10x$? that is, making averages, how long did Shabaka or Tirhakah, respectively, reign before their respective defeats by Sargon and Sennacherib? and in the case of nine other kings, how long did each reign after the latest monumental date concerning him which we moderns have happened to discover? The average highest date for the nine is less than 21 years. It is not unlikely that the average length of their reigns was several years more than that. It is very improbable that in all nine cases the latest date that explorers have happened to find is one near the close of the reign. Certainly the average value of x cannot be less than two or three or four years. In fine, if we could ascertain all the values, it is probable that the additions and the subtractions would nearly balance, leaving the number 998 not greatly changed as that of the year of the accession of Shishak.

If Shishak became king B. C. 998, and if, as has been commonly held, the invasion occurred twenty years later, this date exactly synchronizes with that of the biblical numbers. No significance, however, attaches to the exactness of the synchronism, because there are elements of uncertainty in the Egyptian numeral; but great significance attaches to the point that the Egyptian facts thus indicate a date which cannot possibly be very different from that given in the Bible. Yet more significant is the point that these same Egyptian facts prove the Assyrian date for the same events to be incorrect by several decades.[1]

It is astonishing that Egyptologists should still hold to the correctness of the Assyrian dates for this period. How can they do it? One scholar does it in this way: first, he estimates the Egyptian co-reigns and other overlaps at thirty years, in which he is perhaps correct. Second, he cancels all the x values, tacitly assuming that the last date found on the monuments for any reign indicates the last year of that reign—a false assumption, of course. Third, in contradiction with the Assyrian and the biblical records, he makes the first year of Shabaka to be B. C. 712, and that of Tirhakah B. C. 688. Fourth, he arbitrarily drops 10 years from the minimum dates for the twenty-third dynasty. Arithmetic of this type does not commend itself.

b. It is a simple process to extend this computation back to the time of the eighteenth dynasty, and to test by it the date (May 3, B. C. 1501) assigned for the accession of Thutmose III, noting that the other alleged exact dates of the scheme stand or fall with this. The data, except the first item, are from Professor Breasted.

Beginning of twenty-second dynasty..................B. C.	998 nearly
Twenty-first dynasty, years........................	134 plus $6x$
Twentieth dynasty................................	102 plus $5x$
Interim, "many years"............................	y
Nineteenth dynasty...............................	139 plus $6x$
Eighteenth dynasty from accession of Thutmose...	147 plus $3x$
Accession of Thutmose III.....................B. C.	1520 plus $20x$ plus y

In the numbers for these last four dynasties the reductions for overlapping reigns have already been made, so that no further reductions are in order. No comment is necessary. Putting any value you please upon x, the numerals prove conclusively that the accession of Thutmose was a good many decades before

---

[1] The hypotheses that Sargon's Shabaka was some one earlier than the known king of that name, and that Tirhakah's encounter with Sennacherib occurred before he became king, are unsupported.

B. C. 1501, and consequently that the alleged basis for astronomical computation does not exist.

To this some one will reply that the Assyrian date for the accession of Shishak is to be accepted, even at the cost of rejecting the biblical and Egyptian testimony. Substitute the Assyrian date, about B. C. 947, for the 998 in the above computation, and the result will become B. C. 1469 plus $20x$ plus y. As the value of y is not a few years, but "many years," and as the average value of x can hardly be less than 2 or 3 or 4 years, we still have a minimum far above the B. C. 1501 assigned by the theory for the accession of Thutmose III. This conclusion becomes yet more decided when we look at certain details concerning the twentieth and twenty-first Egyptian dynasties (see 26, 35). Probably the Egyptian Sothic chronology has value, but its true interpretation is yet to be learned.

c. But if the time allowance of the current schemes of Egyptian chronology for this period is thus too small, do not the Egyptian data equally prove that the time allowance in the Bible is much too long?

The common opinion is that the exodus occurred shortly before the close of the nineteenth dynasty. The biblical data give us nearly an even 500 years from then to the accession of Shishak. Professor Breasted's estimate for the same period is about 260 years. Is not the larger number in contradiction with Egyptian facts?

The Egyptian events include the reigns of nineteen or twenty kings, the rule of a Syrian usurper, and "many years" of anarchy. The reports of the total in the different copies of Manetho range from 249 to 308. The monuments show that Manetho's numbers in the case of some of the kings are too small. For the kings, leaving out the usurper and the time of anarchy, Professor Breasted's minimum total of years is $236\frac{1}{2}$ plus $11x$. Certainly this showing does not strikingly confirm the biblical representation, but it does not necessarily contradict it. The 500 years is not an excessively long period for twenty reigns or more. If we knew more about the reigns we should be better qualified to judge. Additional information may show us that the events filled the full 500 years. We shall presently find that the Babylonian long numbers affirm this.

Both now and in the past there have been those who assigned the exodus to some earlier Egyptian dynasty. That is a matter to be decided on its own merits but it is not a necessity in order to the defense of the biblical statements.

26. *Bible Chronology as Compared with the Earlier Babylonian and Assyrian.*—Prominent among the data are the Babylonian lists of kings, and certain long numbers.

a. The lists of kings, existing some centuries before Christ, reckoned eight dynasties before that in which Ptolemy's canon (see 8*c*) begins. Of these lists certain parts are now accessible, partly as the result of piecing together the fragmentary contents of different copies.[1]

---

[1] See books of reference. Very convenient is the account given by Sayce in *Records of the Past*, new series, Vol. I.

Of the first dynasty, that of Hammurabi, the names and years of all the 11 kings, with a mutilated footing. The sum is 304 years.

Of the second dynasty the names and years of all the 11 kings, with the footing 368 years.

Of the third dynasty the names or the years, much mutilated, of 22 of the 36 kings, the middle 14 names being entirely gone; and the footing 576 years and 9 months.

For the fourth dynasty there were 12 lines, giving the names and years of 11 kings, and a footing. There remain the years of the first 2 kings, and mutilated parts of the lines for the last 4, with the footing 72 years and 6 months.

Of the remaining dynasties it is sufficient to say here that the records are too mutilated to give a continuous chronology. At points there is material from other sources for supplementing the lists of the several dynasties.

b. To bridge over the broken places in these lists scholars resort to certain long numbers that are found in the records. The following numbers of this class bear on the period covered by the biblical chronology.

First, Sennacherib says that in B. C. 689 he brought from Babylon certain gods that had been carried there 418 years previously by Marduk-nadin-ahhi, king of Babylon, the contemporary of Tiglath-pilezer I, king of Assyria. Counting inclusively, 689 plus 418 equals 1106; that is, it was in B. C. 1106 that the gods were carried to Babylon, and this gives us a date for these two contemporary kings.

Second, Sennacherib says that at the same date he brought from Babylon the seal of Tukulti-ninip, which had gone there with that king 600 years before. The 600 is a round number, and is doubtless a little larger than the exact number. This gives us a date in the reign of Tukulti-ninip not long after B. C. 1288. The Babylonian contemporary must have been one of the kings whose name has been lost from the lists of the third dynasty.

Third, Nabonidus, B. C. 555–539, says that he rebuilt a temple which had not been rebuilt for 800 years, from the time of Shagashalti-buriash, the son of Kudur-bel, the king. This gives the date about B. C. 1345 for the younger of these two kings of Babylon. Their names are among those that have been lost from the list of the third dynasty.

Fourth, Marduk-nadin-ahhi, mentioned in the first instance above, was probably the king whose mutilated name appears ninth in the list of the fourth dynasty. His reign of 1½ years closed 22 years before the close of the 72½ years of the dynasty. As Tiglath-pilezer claims to have defeated him in two separate campaigns, his victory over Assyria must have been earlier than the defeats, that is, in his accession year.

Accession of Marduk-nadin-ahhi..................................B. C.	1106
Previous years of fourth dynasty (72½ less 24½)..............	48
Third dynasty, years nearly...	577
Second dynasty...	368
First dynasty from the accession of Hammurabi...............	192
Accession of Hammurabi...B. C.	2291

Fifth, Asshur-bani-pal, king of Assyria B. C. 668-626, who had wars with Elam about B. C. 649, says that he brought back to her place the goddess Nana, who had been in exile in Elam 1635 years. The carrying of her to Elam may easily have been an incident of the Elamite wars that marked the earlier part of the reign of Hammurabi, and this agrees well with Asshur-bani-pal's figures, for 649 plus 1635 equals 2284, a date 7 years after that just found for the accession of Hammurabi.

Sixth, Nabonidus[1] informs us that Hammurabi preceded by 700 years Burna-buriash, king of Babylon, the contemporary of Asshur-uballit, king of Assyria, and of Amenhôtep IV of Egypt. Counting from accession to accession, 2291 minus 700 equals 1591, the approximate date in years B. C. of Burna-buriash. As we have here a round number, and considerable room for variation, call this date about B. C. 1600.

According to the long numbers we have therefore a series of dates: B. C. 1106, about B. C. 1288, about B. C. 1345, about B. C. 1600, B. C. 2291. Considerable parts of the chronological line indicated by these points can be filled out in detail, and on the whole the long numbers are confirmed by the details which we possess.

c. But this relatively simple solution of the problem does not at present command a consensus of opinion among scholars. Professor Hommel (*Ancient Hebrew Tradition*, p. 120) gives a table of variant opinions concerning the accession of Hammurabi, in which the dates range from B. C. 1923 to B. C. 2394. In his article on Babylonia in the *Dictionary of the Bible*, he abandons all these numbers, dating Hammurabi B. C. 1772–1717. How shall we account for these differences?

First, Professor Hommel and some others hold, I think correctly, that the third dynasty immediately succeeded the first, the second dynasty being contemporary. This reduces the date of Hammurabi by 368 years. By the figures given above, it becomes B. C. 2291 less 368, that is, B. C. 1923. The 1635 of the fifth instance above and the 700 of the sixth instance are to be similarly reduced, as it is evident that the chronologers counted in the 368 years of the second dynasty. The other long numbers remain unaffected.

Second, the other differences of opinion are due to inferential or conjectural corrections of the data. Especially has conjecture exerted itself, without accomplishing anything like a consensus of opinion, to harmonize these Babylonian and Assyrian data with the alleged Egyptian astronomical chronology (see 24). But there is also a genuine difficulty with the data themselves.

According to the long numbers the accession of Burna-buriash was about 1600 B. C., and that of Tukulti-ninip cannot have been much earlier than 1300 B. C. For the intervening 300 years we know of but five Assyrian kings, and it is incredible that five successive reigns should average sixty years each. The

---

[1] In a document published by C. Bezold in the *Proceedings of the Society of Biblical Archæology*, January 8, 1889, pp. 84ff.

argument is strengthened by the claims made by some of these kings to the relation of father, son, grandson, though it is possible in some of the cases that the terms are used to denote a more remote ancestry. For perhaps the first 120 years of the 300 our information concerning Assyrian history is somewhat full; it is a blank for what the long numbers represent to be the century and a half after that. For that same century and a half our information concerning Babylonia consists mainly in blanks in the list of the third dynasty, supplemented by what Nabonidus says concerning Kudur-bel and Shagashalti-buriash. No wonder that many assume the non-existence of a large part of this century and a half, and try to correct the data accordingly.

d. This becomes more significant when we compare the eastern data with the biblical and the Egyptian. The blank century and a half corresponds in part with the times of the judges, and with those of the twentieth Egyptian dynasty. There is plausibility in the idea that the biblical chronology needs to be shortened at this point. Counting the forties which so abound at this period as round numbers, one might supposably reduce the time by several decades without positively discrediting the Bible numbers.

But no one has done this successfully, and at present there are no sufficient data for doing it accurately. When additional information comes in, it is quite as likely to be of such a nature as to fill out the blank spaces and confirm the long numbers as to be of any other nature. For the present the only thing to do is to record the facts as the testimony gives them. If the testimony is to be corrected, that can be attended to when correcting evidence is found. As the record stands, the date for Hammurabi is B. C. 1923, that for Burna-buriash about 1600, that for Shagashalti-buriash about 1345, that for Tukulti-ninip about 1288, that for Marduk-nadin-ahhi 1106. These numbers are those of the Assyrian chronology. To conform them to the biblical chronology as given in my tables, add in each case 51 years.

27. *A Generalization.*—The principal question at issue between the biblical chronology and the recent adverse schemes is whether the Bible makes the time too long. Does it interpolate 51 years for the times after Solomon? Does it interpolate two centuries and more for the times between Joseph and Solomon? On this question we throw out the argument from the Egyptian Sothic cycle as not having yet been properly connected with the events. This done, all the positive testimony, biblical, Egyptian, Assyrian, Babylonian, favors the longer chronology. All the evidence in favor of the shorter may be resolved into three groups of negative facts.

First, the Assyrian eponym list omits 51 years in the time after Solomon, and the later Assyrian and Babylonian chronologers follow the list as thus shortened. This is merely negative proof, and we found it sharply contradicted by positive facts from Egyptian sources (see 25a) as well as by the Bible.

Second, the lists and accounts we have of the twentieth and twenty-first Egyptian dynasties only account for a part of the time which the biblical records claim between the exodus and Solomon. Again the proof is merely negative. If we had the lists and accounts more in full they might account for more of the time.

Third, for a part of the same period the Assyrian documents, and for a shorter part the Babylonian, fail to fill out all the time called for by the biblical chronology (see 26c, d). Yet again, the fact affords only negative proof. The next news from the Orient may supply some of the missing material. To some extent the Egyptian records are full when the Babylonian are empty, and *vice versa*. It is only for a few decades that both are empty at the same time.

These omissions cannot be accepted as invalidating the positive evidence we possess of the essential correctness of the Bible chronology.

Chapter V

The Tables

28. General Considerations.—*a.* I am afraid that some one will look at these tables and say that they are crowded with details, and too complicated to be of use. If such a one will fix his eye on the columns of events and of the Christian era, he will see that these by themselves constitute the simplest possible table, and that they can be used without paying attention to the rest. If after a time he should take an interest in finding reasons, or in studying differences of opinion, he will find that then the rest of the contents will be of use to him.

b. The tables have of course been made out from the point of view of one who regards the biblical accounts as true history. But one who does not so regard them yet needs to study them in the light of their time data, and to study the problem of their time data itself.

c. The tables are properly tables of Old Testament chronology. The reason for continuing them to include later times is to show the connection of the later times with the Old Testament narrative.

29. The Divisions of the History and of the Chronology.—*a.* The division of the history, as expressed in the Old Testament itself, is into four periods. The first six books sketch what the writers regard as the formative period, terminating with the establishment of Israel and Israel's sanctuary and institutions in the promised land. The books of Judges and Ruth and Samuel sketch the period when the institutions were fluctuating and the sanctuary wandering. The books of Kings treat of the third period, during which they represent that the sanctuary was fixed, was the permanent temple in Jerusalem. Notice that they do not begin with the establishment of the monarchy, nor with David, but with the arrangements for building the temple. The connected series of books known as 1 and 2 Chronicles and Ezra and Nehemiah first makes a review of the three preceding periods, and then treats of a fourth period, that of the postexilian restoration of the sanctuary.

b. The divisions of the chronology are somewhat different. One method prevails for the first period of the history. A second begins, overlapping a little, at the beginning of the second period; and a third begins, not at the close of the second period but at the death of Solomon, and the disruption of the kingdom which followed. It is convenient to treat these divisions of the chronology as three separate though connected eras. The first is the era of the migration of Abraham to Canaan (A. Mig.). The second is the era from the transit of Israel across the Jordan under Joshua (A. T. J.). The third is the era of the disruption of the kingdom (A. Di.).

30. The Columns of Numerals.—The heart of the graphic representation in the tables lies in the columns of numerals in the middle of the right-hand page. The column to the right serves as a standard by which to measure the others, and is printed in heavy-faced type. To the left are other columns, presenting the chronological data as given in the Bible and other sources, and the dates B. C. The number of columns varies, as many being used for any period as the data of that period require.

On each side of the columns are heavy vertical lines, made up of alternating black and white spaces corresponding to the horizontal lines of figures. Each horizontal line represents a year. There are twenty-five lines on a page, that being in many ways a convenient number for use.

Notice in particular the standard column. Many are accustomed to use exclusively the years of the Christian era as a standard for fixing dates. But that is always inconvenient for the times before the beginning of the era, because of the processes of subtraction which it requires; and it becomes particularly inconvenient when we get back to the times when the dates in years B. C. are in dispute. For these reasons, though I have extended a B. C. column throughout the tables, I have not made that the standard for the earlier times, but have used for that purpose the years of the three eras into which Old Testament chronology naturally divides itself. It is convenient to note that the black spaces in the heavy vertical lines are opposite the odd years in the standard, and the white spaces opposite the even years. The years B. C., though provisional for the earlier centuries, serve to bind the three eras together into a continuous course of time.

31. *The Explanatory Columns.*—*a.* In the wide column to the right of the numerals are placed the dated Israelitish events mentioned in the history, each event opposite the numeral which indicates its date. An interrogation point indicates that the dating is only a probable inference, or a conjecture.

b. The wide column to the left of the numerals is a similar record of synchronous events in other nations than Israel.

c. The right-hand column of the left-hand page is a résumé, with references, of the biblical statements that contain the dates. In the left-hand column are placed such additional matters as it has seemed best to present.

32. *The Use of the Tables.*—They present to the eye a complete topical list of the dated events of the history, arranged in the order of time, together with the dates of the events and the intervals by which they were separated.

In the right-hand column select any event and follow the line across the page, and you will find its date in terms of a biblical era; the numbers that justify that date; its actual or provisional date in terms B. C.; synchronous events in other nations; the biblical or other data on which these conclusions are based.

Necessarily some of the pages are crowded, while others are nearly blank. But this is in itself an important part of the presentation to the eye. Nothing could more sharply distinguish the eventful parts of the history from the uneventful.

33. *Accession Dates.*—It is a necessity of the plan of tabulation that in the tables the numeral 1 stands opposite the "first year" of a king; not opposite

his "accession year," unless that is also counted as his first year (see 19*b*). Most writers give dates from the accession year, which is commonly the year before the first year. Hence there is often a difference of one year between the number given in the tables and the number as commonly stated, but the difference is only apparent, and not real.

34. *Comparison with Other Schemes; the Later Times.*—Most of the differences are treated in the places where they occur. A few of the most important are grouped together here.

a. Back to the fall of Samaria there should be no chronological differences except in matters of detail. At that point there is a difference, though there is really no room for it. The biblical numbers give the date as B. C. 718, as any one may see by adding them. Ussher's millennial scheme (see below) led him to stretch the time, at this point, to "about" B. C. 721. This has led many to regard Sargon's capture of the city in B. C. 722 as its final capture, in spite of his saying that Samaria was two years later in alliance with other nations against him. The traditional false date is still very commonly given, and is very misleading.

b. From the downfall of Samaria back to the accession of Amaziah the differences are more important. Many of my dates differ from those of Ussher by either 4 or 7 or 11 years. Ussher supposed that he knew it to be a fact that just 1000 years elapsed between the dedication of the temple and the birth of Jesus. The Bible numbers taken at their most obvious values make the interval 1007 years. Quite plausibly, he interprets the date of the accession of Uzziah (2 Ki. 15: 1) by assuming a co-reign of Jeroboam II with his predecessor, and thus shortens the period by 11 years. Later he gets back 4 of the 11 years, thus making his thousand an even one. In this it seems to me that he is mistaken.

It is in this period that the conflict comes in between the biblical and the Assyrian chronology (see above, 23). For this period I add, for comparison, a column giving the dates B. C. on the Assyrian basis.

Back from Amaziah to Solomon my dates should be reducible to those of Ussher by subtracting 7, and to the Assyrian by subtracting 51.

c. For the reign of David the tables have considerable that is distinctive. His $40\frac{1}{2}$ years were 41 years by the more common way of counting. He reigned one year after his fortieth year (2 Sam. 15: 7; 1 Chron. 26: 31). Absalom's rebellion occurred in David's forty-first year, and most of the preparations for the temple occurred earlier. The bringing up of the ark to Jerusalem was after David's conquests and his great sin. See the details in the notes on the tables. The chronology is of course affected by these views as to the order of the events.

35. *Comparison with Other Schemes; the Middle Period.*—As my tables add 7 to Ussher's date for the disruption of the kingdom, so of course they continue to add the 7 for all the time previous. They also differ from Ussher in recognizing the separate block of the chronology found in the forty-year periods when the land was "quiet" (Jud. 3: 11, 30, 5: 31, 8: 28). In this block the other numbers used are included in the forty-year periods.

The question arises whether there are four of these periods or five; that is, whether the eighty in Judges 3:30 does or does not include the preceding forty, With this goes the question whether the 480 in 1 Kings 6:1 is counted from the beginning of the 40 years of the exodus, or from the end. I have heretofore expressed in print the opinion that there were five of these periods, and that the count in Kings is from the close of the exodus period. It now seems to me safer, however, to follow the shorter count, especially as there is in any case a provisional element in the results reached.

For the period from Joshua to Solomon some chronologists have demanded a much longer time, while the prevailing feature of the modern schemes is to shorten the biblical computation by two centuries or more.

We have already considered this in our discussion of the Egyptian and Babylonian chronologies (above, 24, 25, 26). The 480 years (1 Ki. 6:1) cannot be greatly shortened except on the basis of the wholesale rejection of the biblical numbers.

36. *Comparison with Other Schemes; the Earlier Times.*—For the times before the death of Moses the differences of opinion are wide.

a. Except as modifying elements enter, my dates for this period may be reduced to those of Ussher by subtracting 7. For comparison with dates drawn exclusively from Assyrian or Babylonian sources, the tabular numbers should be reduced by 51, with modifying elements in some instances.

b. My tables agree with Ussher in regarding the 430 years of the sojourn in Egypt (Ex. 12:40, 41) as beginning when Abraham came to Canaan. This is the traditional interpretation, explicitly stated in the Septuagint and Josephus, and apparently followed by Paul (Gal. 3:17). The 400 of Genesis 15:13 seems to be a round number to the same effect, beginning at about the time when the message was given to Abraham. This way of counting, in which the initial terminus is left to inference, is not unknown in the Bible (see 19*d*). "The fourth generation" of Genesis 15:16 is to be interpreted by such a succession as Levi, Kohath, Amram, Aaron, or Kohath, Amram, Aaron, Eleazar, successions in which four exceptional generations actually spanned the time of the sojourn in Egypt.

Some scholars, however, count the 430 years as occupied with the actual sojourn in Egypt, thus lengthening the whole period by more than 200 years.

c. Among scholars who regard Abraham as a historical person there is a very general consensus to the effect that he was contemporary with Hammurabi, the distinguished king of Babylonia, the Amraphel of Genesis 14 (see 26).[1]

The Assyrian and Babylonian long numbers, uncorrected, give us B. C. 1923 Assyrian, that is, B. C. 1974 in my tables, as the first year of Hammurabi (see 26*b*). On this basis the migration of Abraham to Palestine was

---

[1] On Hammurabi and Abraham see, among other works, Hommel's *Ancient Hebrew Tradition*; Pinches, *Old Testament in the Light of the Historical Records of Assyria and Babylon*; Clay, *Light on the Old Testament from Babel*.

in the forty-sixth year of Hammurabi. One could assign plausible reasons for correcting the data somewhere, so as to put the migration earlier in Hammurabi's reign. But the data for a well-founded correction are lacking. As matters stand, one should not be too dogmatic as to the dates B. C. In any case the synchronism is real.

37. *Corollaries.*—*a.* The biblical chronology is not yet superseded. Irrespective of religious questions it deserves to be carefully studied, if only for the light it throws on the results of modern explorations.

b. There is no biblical chronology for the times before Abraham. The pre-Abrahamic tables of numbers (Gen. 5 and 11: 10–25) are ethnical and not biographical, and we have no key to the duration of time intended in them. On the basis of the Babylonian long numbers, and on other grounds, it is now commonly held that there were civilizations in the valleys of the Euphrates and of the Nile some thousands of years before Abraham.

c. Our chronological results are valuable even when they are more or less provisional. For the times before the downfall of Samaria there is no agreement among scholars as to the dates in years B. C. of the Old Testament events, and many of the dates commonly given are misleading. The further back we go the more pronounced are the differences. For the times of the judges scholars differ by hundreds of years, and yet more for the time of the sojourn in Egypt and for the earlier times. Nevertheless, in most cases the order of even the earlier events can be ascertained, and they can be dated relatively to each other and to events occurring in foreign nations, even when these dates cannot be fixed in the terms of our era. We can find blocks of correctly known chronology, even when the blocks are not continuous. Synchronisms constitute the most important element in chronology, and the synchronisms given in my tables ought to be accepted, most of them, even by persons who hold different theories as to the dates in years B. C.

38. For the Assyrian, Babylonian, and Egyptian matters in this volume I have made many references to the series of little books entitled *Records of the Past*, to George Smith's *Assyrian Canon* and *Assyrian Discoveries*, and to Schrader. I hope that I have not in any instance failed to verify my statements by more recent works. I have retained these references, partly for the convenience of using notes made long ago, but principally because in these volumes one can go as near to the original sources as an honest translation brings him, and because I suppose that these are still the most accessible works in English which will enable one to do this.

TABLES

OF

OLD TESTAMENT CHRONOLOGY

FIRST TABLE

ABRAHAM TO JOSHUA

Notes.

In explanation of the Tables see Introduction, especially Chapter V.

a The column B. C. is marked with an interrogation point as being provisional (Int. Chap. IV). The proof for the numbers given consists in tracing them back from some point that is undisputed, B. C. 604 for example.

The years contemplated in the tables are vernal years, beginning in March, at a new moon near the spring equinox (Int. Chap. III).

b The abbreviation A. Mig. stands for *Anno Migrationis*, the year of Abraham's migration to Canaan (Int. 29*b*, 30, 31).

c The numbers in the column headed "Abraham" denote the years of Abraham's age.

d A. Mig. 8. On this occasion Abraham raised 318 men (Gen. 14:14). The narrative throughout represents him as at the head of a considerable clan.

e A. Mig. 9. For the numerals (Gen. 15:13, 16) see Introduction 36*b*.

Explanations of the Dates.

Abraham came to Canaan when he was 75 years old (Gen. 12:4).

His going to Egypt must have been at an early date following.

His separation from Lot must have been some years after they came to Canaan, and some years before Lot became permanently identified with Sodom.

Abimelech's attempt to marry Sarah must have occurred before some of the events of Chapter 19, and is to be placed as early as possible. The writer first finishes what he has to say concerning Lot, and then returns to this earlier incident.

The marriage with Hagar was after 10 years' residence in Canaan (Gen. 16:3).

Ishmael was born when Abraham was 86 years old (Gen. 16:16). Compare 99 minus 13 (Gen. 17:24, 25).

At the circumcision Abraham was 99 years old, and Isaac was to be born when Abraham was 100 (Gen. 17:1, 17, 24, 21), the season after the theophany at Mamre (Gen. 18:10, 14), which occurred just before the destruction of Sodom. The three events belong to the same year, or practically the same.

THE TABLES

Foreign Dated Events.	? B.C. *a*	Abraham. *c*	A. Mig. *b*	Israelitish Dated Events.
Shepherd kings in Egypt, as is shown by Abraham's reception there.	1928	75	1	Abraham's first year in Canaan (Gen. 12:1-9).
	1927	76	2	? Abraham in Egypt (Gen. 12:10-20).
	1926	77	3	
	1925	78	4	
Hammurabi (Amraphel), king of Babylonia, which has recently become powerful by the consolidation of smaller states. Ur and Larsa (Ellasar) and other kingdoms have become either subject or tributary, and Elam has been reduced from a superior to a subordinate position.	1924	79	5	? Separation of Lot from Abraham (Gen. 13).
	1923	80	6	? Abimelech takes Sarah (Gen. 20).
	1922	81	7	
	1921	82	8	? Abraham rescues Lot *d* (Gen. 14). ? Melchizedek (Gen. 14:18-22).
	1920	83	9	? The covenant of the parts *e* (Gen. 15).
	1919	84	10	Abraham marries Hagar (Gen. 16).
	1918	85	11	
	1917	86	12	Ishmael born (Gen. 16:4-16).
	1916	87	13	
	1915	88	14	
	1914	89	15	
	1913	90	16	
	1912	91	17	
	1911	92	18	
	1910	93	19	
	1909	94	20	
	1908	95	21	
	1907	96	22	
	1906	97	23	
	1905	98	24	
	1904	99	25	Covenant of circumcision (Gen. 17). Theophany at Mamre (Gen. 18). Destruction of Sodom (Gen. 19).

Notes.

a A. Mig. 28. It does not follow from the sending away of Ishmael that Abraham broke off relations with him. It was necessary that the tribe should not be torn by doubts as to who should succeed Abraham as its chief, but doubtless Abraham made provision for Ishmael as his son (cf. Gen. 25:6), and for Hagar as well. It was tragedy for Hagar, but there is no reason for giving a needlessly harsh interpretation to the incident.

Explanations of the Dates.

Isaac was born when Abraham was 100 years old (Gen. 21:5).

The sending away of Ishmael occurred at the weaning of Isaac, and before Ishmael was full grown. He was not so heavy but that his mother could carry him (21:15). Two years after the birth of Isaac answers these conditions.

The dates for the covenant with Abimelech and for the birth of Moab and Ammon are purely conjectural, except that the events occurred at some time in these years.

Ishmael was of course grown up when he married (Gen. 21:21). Beyond that the date is conjectural.

At the time of the sacrifice Isaac was old enough to carry the wood (ver. 6), a rather heavy load. In the absence of other evidence I have followed Josephus (*Ant.* I. xiii, 2), who says that Isaac was then 25 years old.

THE TABLES

FOREIGN DATED EVENTS.	? B. C.	ISAAC.	ABRAHAM.	A. MIG.	ISRAELITISH DATED EVENTS.
	1903	1	100	26	The birth of Isaac (Gen. 21).
	1902	2	101	27	
	1901	3	102	28	? Ishmael sent away a (Gen. 21: 8-21).
	1900	4	103	29	? Covenant with Abimelech (Gen. 21: 22–34).
	1899	5	104	30	? Moab and Ammon born (Gen. 19: 30–38).
	1898	6	105	31	
Shepherd kings in Egypt, and kings of the dynasty of Hammurabi in Babylon.	1897	7	106	32	
	1896	8	107	33	
	1895	9	108	34	? Ishmael marries an Egyptian wife.
	1894	10	109	35	
	1893	11	110	36	
Ishmael begins gathering a clan akin to that of Abraham, but independent.	1892	12	111	37	
	1891	13	112	38	
	1890	14	113	39	
	1889	15	114	40	
	1888	16	115	41	
	1887	17	116	42	
	1886	18	117	43	
	1885	19	118	44	
	1884	20	119	45	
	1883	21	120	46	
	1882	22	121	47	
	1881	23	122	48	
	1880	24	123	49	
	1879	25	124	50	? The Isaac sacrifice (Gen. 22).

Notes

a A. Mig. 63. The narrative affirms that Sarah, Abraham, Isaac, Jacob, Levi, Joseph, Moses and others attained to an extraordinary old age. It does not represent that people generally lived longer then than now. The instances of great longevity are clearly individual and exceptional, though the biblical writers evidently think of the stock as being exceptional for robustness and length of life.

Explanations of the Dates

We have tolerably definite information as to the length of the reigns of the eighteenth and nineteenth Egyptian dynasties. Assuming that the exodus was near the close of the nineteenth dynasty, and that its date was B. C. 1498 (B. C. 1447 by the Assyrian reckoning), we can assign dates to the Egyptian kings that are approximately true *on these assumptions*. On the basis of these dates, it will be found, the biblical and the Egyptian events in many cases fit very closely. Of course dates of this kind have a wide margin of variation.

Sarah died at the age of 127 years (Gen. 23:1). As she was 10 years younger than Abraham (Gen. 17:17), this was when he was 137 years old.

Isaac married at the age of 40 years (Gen. 25:20).

To give time for Keturah's sons (Gen. 25:1-6) to grow up before Abraham's death, we must assume that he married Keturah soon after the death of Sarah.

THE TABLES

Foreign Dated Events.	? B. C.	Isaac.	Abraham.	A. Mig.	Israelitish Dated Events.
	1878	26	125	51	
	1877	27	126	52	
	1876	28	127	53	
	1875	29	128	54	
	1874	30	129	55	
	1873	31	130	56	
	1872	32	131	57	
	1871	33	132	58	
	1870	34	133	59	
	1869	35	134	60	
Kings of the Hammurabi dynasty in Babylon. Ammiditana claims to be "adda (suzerain?) of the Amorite region," as Hammurabi and his Elamite predecessors had been.	1868	36	135	61	
	1867	37	136	62	
	1866	38	137	63	Death of Sarah. *a* Purchase of a burial place (Gen. 23).
	1865	39	138	64	? Abraham marries Keturah.
The clans of Moab and Ammon beginning to form east of the Jordan.	1864	40	139	65	Isaac marries Rebekah (Gen. 24).
	1863	41	140	66	
	1862	42	141	67	
	1861	43	142	68	
About this time the expulsion of the shepherd kings in Egypt, and the beginning of the eighteenth dynasty.	1860	44	143	69	
	1859	45	144	70	
	1858	46	145	71	
	1857	47	146	72	
	1856	48	147	73	
	1855	49	148	74	
	1854	50	149	75	

Notes.

a A. Mig. 100. The conception of Abraham or Jacob or Ishmael or Midian or Sheba or Dedan (Gen. 25: 1–5) as the originator of a clan is not that the person thus named is the lineal progenitor of all the members of the clan. He is rather their father in the sense of being leader and protector. Some of Abraham's sons were men of force and ability. Aided by the powerful influence of his father and kindred, one of these young men would gather followers around him, and his following would ultimately become an important clan or group of clans.

Explanations of the Dates

The twins Esau and Jacob were born when Isaac was 60 years old (Gen. 25: 26).

Before his death, which took place when he was 175 years old (Gen. 25: 7), Abraham made provision for "the sons of the concubines," "and he sent them away from Isaac, his son . . . unto the east country" (Gen. 25: 6). The sons of Hagar and Keturah must be here intended. The narrative does not say that Abraham attended to this business all at once. Presumably, he made the provision for Ishmael some decades earlier than for the others. Not long before his death he made similar provision for the sons of Keturah, perhaps making it anticipative in the case of the younger of them. He dealt with them in a fatherly way, and yet prevented their contesting the claims of Isaac.

THE TABLES

Foreign Dated Events.	? B.C.	Jacob	Isaac	Abraham	A. Mig.	Israelitish Dated Events.
	1853		51	150	76	
	1852		52	151	77	
	1851		53	152	78	
	1850		54	153	79	
	1849		55	154	80	
	1848		56	155	81	
	1847		57	156	82	
	1846		58	157	83	
	1845		59	158	84	
	1844	1	60	159	85	Birth of Jacob and Esau (Gen. 25 : 19-34).
Kings of the Hammurabi dynasty in Babylon, and the early kings of the eighteenth dynasty in Egypt. The supremacy over the Mediterranean region passing from Babylonia to Egypt.	1843	2	61	160	86	
	1842	3	62	161	87	
	1841	4	63	162	88	
	1840	5	64	163	89	
	1839	6	65	164	90	
	1838	7	66	165	91	
	1837	8	67	166	92	
	1836	9	68	167	93	
	1835	10	69	168	94	
	1834	11	70	169	95	
The sons of Keturah, including at this time or later such clan chiefs as Medan and Midian and Sheba and Dedan, are forming clans in the "east country," in affiliation with the Ishmaelites who have preceded them thither.	1833	12	71	170	96	
	1832	13	72	171	97	
	1831	14	73	172	98	
	1830	15	74	173	99	? Abraham completes his arrangements for the sons of Hagar and Keturah *a* (Gen. 25: 1-18).
	1829	16	75	174	100	

NOTES.

a A. Mig. 102. Whichever son had the birthright would be second in command during Isaac's life, and chief of the clan after Isaac's death.

b A. Mig. 103. The incident of Abimelech and Rebekah (Gen. 26: 7–11) is like two incidents in the life of Sarah (Gen. 12: 11–20, 20: 2–18); and Isaac's covenant with Abimelech, connected with the name Beersheba, is paralleled in the narrative concerning Abraham (Gen. 26 : 26–33, 21 : 22–34). There is no reason in either case for regarding the narratives as mere variations of the same story. Such incidents, if they occurred at all, were likely to repeat themselves.

In Genesis 21 and 26 the region is called the land of the Philistines, and the people are called Philistines. Possibly the term is here used only in a geographical sense, the Philistines proper coming in later. See at A. Mig. 444.

EXPLANATIONS OF THE DATES.

Abraham was 175 years old at his death (Gen. 25: 7).

From the order of the narrative we infer that the birthright incident occurred before the sojourn in Gerar. Perhaps Abraham's death set the boys to thinking of the birthright.

Esau married when he was 40 years old (Gen. 26: 34).

THE TABLES

FOREIGN DATED EVENTS.	? B. C.	JACOB.	ISAAC.	ABRAHAM.	A. MIG.	ISRAELITISH DATED EVENTS.
	1828	17	76	175	101	? Death of Abraham (Gen. 25: 7–11).
	1827	18	77		102	? The affair of the birthright *a* (Gen. 25: 27–34).
Egypt was now under the kings of the eighteenth dynasty, who would not have received Isaac kindly.	1826	19	78		103	? Famine. Isaac forbidden to go to Egypt and dwells long at Gerar *b* (Gen. 26).
	1825	20	79		104	
	1824	21	80		105	
	1823	22	81		106	
	1822	23	82		107	
	1821	24	83		108	
	1820	25	84		109	
	1819	26	85		110	
	1818	27	86		111	
Kings of the Hammurabi dynasty in Babylon.	1817	28	87		112	
	1816	29	88		113	
	1815	30	89		114	
	1814	31	90		115	
	1813	32	91		116	
	1812	33	92		117	
	1811	34	93		118	
	1810	35	94		119	
	1809	36	95		120	
	1808	37	96		121	
	1807	38	97		122	
	1806	39	98		123	
	1805	40	99		124	Esau marries Hittite wives.
	1804	41	100		125	

NOTES.

a A. Mig. 145. Presumably Isaac intended the blessing as a formal recognition of Esau as having the birthright. He regarded Jacob's purchase of it as null, and meant to prevent contention after his death. Note that Jacob obtained no possession of the birthright till after he had made restitution to Esau, nor until Esau abandoned it (Gen. 36:6) after Isaac's death.

b It is common to assume that Jacob's 6 years of service for cattle followed without interval his 14 years of service for his wives (Gen. 31:41, 38 cf. 29:18, 20, 27, 30); but this is not explicitly asserted in the narrative, and the facts show it to be impossible.

In the table I have averaged the intervals between the births of Leah's children at two years, and have conjectured four years for the interval during which she was not bearing.

EXPLANATIONS OF THE DATES.

Jacob's fraud for the blessing was committed just before he went to Paddan-aram. The date of his going thither is fixed by the fact that he was 130 years old when he went to Egypt (Gen. 47:9). For details look up that date, and trace the dates back from it, in the tables. Joseph was 38 when Jacob was 130; Dinah was a young lady when Joseph was 6 years old; Leah bore six children older than Dinah, besides an interval when "she left off bearing." These facts fix a minimum for the time. The maximum is fixed by the fact that Rachel bore a son after the return to Canaan. Jacob's waiting 7 years for her suggests that she was but a child when they first met. *b*

Esau's alliance with Ishmael was probably not delayed long after Jacob's departure. Probably, though not necessarily, it took place before Ishmael himself died at the age of 137 (Gen. 25:17). As Ishmael was born A. Mig. 12, this would be. A Mig. 148.

THE TABLES

Foreign Dated Events.	? B.C.	Jacob.	Isaac.	A. Mig.	Israelitish Dated Events.
	1803	42	101	126	
	1802	43	102	127	
	1801	44	103	128	
	1800	45	104	129	
	1799	46	105	130	
	1798	47	106	131	
	1797	48	107	132	
	1796	49	108	133	
	1795	50	109	134	
	1794	51	110	135	
Kings of the eighteenth dynasty in Egypt.	1793	52	111	136	
	1792	53	112	137	
	1791	54	113	138	
	1790	55	114	139	
	1789	56	115	140	
The clan of Ishmael has by this time attained to some standing.	1788	57	116	141	
	1787	58	117	142	
	1786	59	118	143	
	1785	60	119	144	? The affair of the blessing a (Gen. 27).
	1784	61	120	145	? Jacob goes to Paddan-aram b (Gen. 27: 41–29: 14).
About this time the close of the Hammurabi dynasty in Babylon. Succeeded by the Kassite dynasty.	1783	62	121	146	? Esau's Ishmaelite marriages (Gen. 28: 6–9).
	1782	63	122	147	? Jacob's first year with Laban (Gen. 29: 14–17).
	1781	64	123	148	Death of Ishmael.
	1780	65	124	149	
	1779	66	125	150	

NOTES.

a A. Mig. 159. After his 14 years of service for his two wives Jacob seems to have had a period of drifting. Doubtless he remained with Laban, but he was a demoralized man, and he afterward counted these years as nothing. He was recalled to self-respect by Jehovah's kindness to him in giving him Joseph.

EXPLANATIONS OF THE DATES.

By way of reasons for the dates see references in the table, and the explanations and notes on the preceding pages.

THE TABLES

Foreign Dated Events.	? B. C.	Jacob.	Isaac.	A. Mig.	Israelitish Dated Events.
	1778	67	126	151	
	1777	68	127	152	? Jacob's 7th year of service for Rachel.
	1776	69	128	153	? Jacob marries Leah and Rachel (Gen. 29: 20 ff).
	1775	70	129	154	? Birth of Reuben (Gen. 29: 32).
	1774	71	130	155	? Birth of Simeon (33).
	1773	72	131	156	
	1772	73	132	157	? Birth of Levi (34).
	1771	74	133	158	
	1770	75	134	159	? 14th year of service of Jacob. *a* ? Birth of Judah (35).
Kings of the Kassite dynasty in Babylonia, and of the eighteenth dynasty in Egypt.	1769	76	135	160	? Leah's years of waiting begin (35) ? Dan born of Bilhah (Gen. 30: 1–6)
	1768	77	136	161	? Gad born of Zilpah (9–11).
	1767	78	137	162	? Naphtali born of Bilhah (7–8).
	1766	79	138	163	? Asher born of Zilpah (12–13).
	1765	80	139	164	? Reuben and the mandrakes (14–16). ? Issachar born of Leah (17–18).
	1764	81	140	165	
	1763	82	141	166	? Zebulun born of Leah (19–20).
	1762	83	142	167	
	1761	84	143	168	? Dinah born (21).
	1760	85	144	169	
	1759	86	145	170	
	1758	87	146	171	
	1757	88	147	172	
	1756	89	148	173	
	1755	90	149	174	
	1754	91	150	175	

NOTES.

a A. Mig. 182. This scene, in which Jacob and all his heirs join in acknowledging Esau as lord, that is, in renouncing all claim to the birthright, has been strangely neglected in estimating the story.

b A. Mig. 193. When Jacob came back from Paddan-aram he found the Shechem and Dothan region agricultural, with flourishing cities. A few years later, when Joseph went there to see his brothers, the region seems to have been a pasturage wilderness, with dry cisterns and other evidences of former prosperity. Doubtless it had been devastated, either by the Egyptians or by their opponents, in some of the wars of Thutmose III.

EXPLANATIONS OF THE DATES.

Joseph was 30 years old the first of the 7 years of plenty (Gen. 41:46). Therefore he was 38 the second year of the famine that followed those seven years, and Jacob was that year 130 years old (Gen. 45:6, 47:9). This gives us the first year of the life of Joseph.

The six years of service for cattle (Gen. 31:41).

The hostile treatment of Shechem preceded the solemnity at Bethel and the birth of Benjamin (Gen. 35:5). Rachel was already pregnant with Benjamin, while on the way to Palestine (Gen. 31:34–35).

To allow room for the other events of Chapter 38, we must place the marriage of Judah and the birth of Er as soon as possible after Jacob's return to Palestine.

Joseph was 17 when taken to Egypt (Gen. 37:2).

THE TABLES

Foreign Dated Events.	? B. C.	Joseph.	Jacob.	Isaac.	A. Mig.	Israelitish Dated Events.
About this time the wars, for 20 years, in which Thutmose III subjugated the peoples from the Mediterranean to beyond the Euphrates, and afterward punished them for attempting to throw off the yoke.	1753		92	151	176	
	1752	1	93	152	177	Birth of Joseph. The first of Jacob's 6 years of service for cattle (Gen. 30:22 ff).
	1751	2	94	153	178	Sixth year. To shearing time (Gen. 31:1-19).
	1750	3	95	154	179	Return to Palestine (Gen. 31: 20 ff).
	1749	4	96	155	180	Reconciliation with Esau a (Gen. 32 and 33).
	1748	5	97	156	181	Shechem and Dinah (Gen. 34). ? Judah marries Bath-shua (Gen. 38).
	1747	6	98	157	182	Solemnity at Bethel (Gen. 35: 1-15).
	1746	7	99	158	183	Birth of Benjamin and death of Rachel (Gen. 35:16-20).
	1745	8	100	159	184	? Birth of Er (Gen. 38:3).
	1744	9	101	160	185	? Birth of Onan (Gen. 38:4).
	1743	10	102	161	186	
Kings of the Kassite dynasty in Babylon.	1742	11	103	162	187	
	1741	12	104	163	188	
	1740	13	105	164	189	
	1739	14	106	165	190	
	1738	15	107	166	191	
The clans of Ishmael and Midian and Medan, under the generic name Ishmaelite (Gen. 37:25, 27, 28, 36 and 39:1).	1737	16	108	167	192	
	1736	17	109	168	193	Joseph taken to Egypt b (Gen. 37).
	1735	18	110	169	194	Joseph in Potiphar's house (Gen. 39).
	1734	19	111	170	195	
	1733	20	112	171	196	
	1732	21	113	172	197	
	1731	22	114	173	198	
	1730	23	115	174	199	
	1729	24	116	175	200	

NOTES.

a A. Mig. 205. Esau's great wealth after Isaac's death was doubtless his inheritance from Isaac. The birthright was still in his possession. Practically he lost it by going to Seir (Gen. 36: 6) where his interests became amalgamated with those of the relatives of his wives.

b A. Mig. 206. Joseph was not made grand vizier, but simply head of the corn storage department. Other heads of departments were like him second in rank only to the king.

Just now some persons are persistent in speaking of Joseph's Pharaoh as one of the shepherd kings. A dozen points in the narrative are inconsistent with this. For example, horses abound, a shepherd is an abomination to the Egyptians, the native priesthood is in high favor.

c A. Mig. 214. Interpret the statement that 70 persons went to Egypt by the details found in Genesis 46. Probably the tribe included some thousands in all, the seventy being those who, later, came to be counted as heads genealogically.

EXPLANATIONS OF THE DATES.

Er was not old enough to marry much earlier than A. Mig. 203, and the marriage was not much later than that if Perez and Zerah (Gen. 38: 27–30) were born before the going to Egypt. (Gen. 46 : 12).

Joseph's two years (or more) in prison directly preceded his exaltation, at the age of 30 years (Gen. 41: 1, 46).

Isaac died at 180 years of age. Esau's moving to Seir seems to have been soon after.

Kohath's birth is of interest for tracing the four generations that spanned the sojourn in Egypt. The date given is provisional, obtained by averaging (Ex. 6: 16, 18, 20).

Jacob was 130 years old when the tribe went to Egypt (Gen. 47: 9).

Apparently, Leah went to Egypt with her thirty-two descendants (Gen. 46: 15). Jacob buried her at Machpelah (Gen. 49: 31), probably not long after.

Foreign Dated Events.	? B. C.	Joseph.	Jacob.	Isaac.	A. Mig.	Israelitish Dated Events.
	1728	25	117	176	201	
	1727	26	118	177	202	
	1726	27	119	178	203	? Er marries Tamar.
	1725	28	120	179	204	Joseph 2 years in prison (Gen. 39–40).
	1724	29	121	180	205	Death of Isaac (Gen. 35: 28–29) Esau finally goes to Seir *a* (Gen. 36).
	1723	30	122		206	Joseph exalted *b* (Gen. 41).
	1722	31	123		207	First of the 7 years of plenty.
	1721	32	124		208	
	1720	33	125		209	
Kings of the Kassite dynasty in Babylonia. Perhaps Amenhotep II of the eighteenth dynasty in Egypt.	1719	34	126		210	
	1718	35	127		211	Seventh of the years of plenty.
	1717	36	128		212	? Perez and Zerah born (38: 6–30).
	1716	37	129		213	First year of famine. ? Kohath born.
	1715	38	130		214	Jacob and his clan go to Egypt *c* (Gen. 42–47).
	1714	39	131		215	
	1713	40	132		216	
	1712	41	133		217	? Death and burial of Leah.
	1711	42	134		218	
	1710	43	135		219	Seventh year of famine.
	1709	44	136		220	
	1708	45	137		221	
	1707	46	138		222	
	1706	47	139		223	
	1705	48	140		224	
	1704	49	141		225	

Notes.

a A. Mig. 231. The narrative represents that Jacob's funeral cortège made a circuitous march, arriving at Hebron from "beyond Jordan" (Gen. 50:10). Supposably this may be accounted for by the rebellions and other disturbances which attended the accession of Thutmose IV. These may have just then taken such a form as to render the shorter route impracticable.

Explanations of the Dates.

Jacob died at the age of 147 years (Gen. 47:28). After his death few notable events are mentioned for several generations.

THE TABLES

Foreign Dated Events.	B.C.	Joseph.	Jacob.	A. Mig.	Israelitish Dated Events.
	1703	50	142	226	
	1702	51	143	227	
	1701	52	144	228	
	1700	53	145	229	
About this time, perhaps, Amenhotep II succeeded by Thutmose IV.	1699	54	146	230	
	1698	55	147	231	Death and burial of Jacob a (Gen. 48–50).
	1697	56		232	
	1696	57		233	
	1695	58		234	
	1694	59		235	
	1693	60		236	
Kings of the Kassite dynasty in Babylon.	1692	61		237	Israel in Egypt.
	1691	62		238	
	1690	63		239	
	1689	64		240	
	1688	65		241	
	1687	66		242	
	1686	67		243	
	1685	68		244	
	1684	69		245	
	1683	70		246	
	1682	71		247	
	1681	72		248	
	1680	73		249	
	1679	74		250	

| NOTES. | EXPLANATIONS OF THE DATES. |

a B. C. 1671. The wide international movement revealed in the Amarna letters is of great interest.

b A. Mig. 261. The representation is that during the sojourn Israel had especial though not exclusive possession of the land of Goshen, in the Nile delta; and that in Goshen they mainly retained the character of sheep and cattle farmers. But the accounts also imply that the Israelites, as they became numerous, spread elsewhere in Egypt, perhaps engaging in other occupations.

THE TABLES

Foreign Dated Events.	? B.C.	Joseph.	A. Mig.	Israelitish Dated Events.
	1678	75	251	
	1677	76	252	
	1676	77	253	
	1675	78	254	
	1674	79	255	
	1673	80	256	
	1672	81	257	
About this time correspondence, preserved in the Amarna letters, between Kallimmasin, king of Babylon, and Amenhotep III, king of Egypt. *a*	1671	82	258	
	1670	83	259	
	1669	84	260	
	1668	85	261	Israel in Egypt. *b*
Also correspondence between Egypt and nations to the north.	1667	86	262	
	1666	87	263	
	1665	88	264	
	1664	89	265	
	1663	90	266	
	1662	91	267	
	1661	92	268	
	1660	93	269	
	1659	94	270	
	1658	95	271	
	1657	96	272	
	1656	97	273	
	1655	98	274	
	1654	99	275	

Notes.

a B. C. 1652. For the date of Burnaburiash see the Introduction (26*b*, Sixth, and context). The date there given is about B. C. 1600 Assyrian, which is about 1650 by the chronology of these tables.

Amenhotep IV is often spoken of as "the heretic king." He substituted the worship of Aton for that of Amon. After 5 years he took the name Ikhn-aton. He built a new capital at Amarna, changing from Thebes. Owing perhaps to religious opposition, his reign was weak, and there was a great falling away of the peoples to the east and northeast of the Mediterranean.

Explanations of the Dates.

The birth of Amram has the same sort of interest in the chronology with that of Kohath (see at A. Mig. 213 and 293).

Joseph was 110 years old at his death.

Levi died at the age of 137 years (Ex. 6: 16).

THE TABLES

FOREIGN DATED EVENTS.	? B. C.	JOSEPH.	A. MIG.	ISRAELITISH DATED EVENTS.
	1653	100	276	
About this time letters from Burna-buriash, king of Babylon, and Asshur-uballit, king of Assyria, to Amenhotep IV, king of Egypt. Several letters are preserved in the Amarna collection. *a*	1652	101	277	
	1651	102	278	
	1650	103	279	
	1649	104	280	? Birth of Amram.
	1648	105	281	
Letters also from Palestine showing a general prevalence of dissatisfaction with Egyptian rule, and much demoralization..	1647	106	282	
	1646	107	283	
	1645	108	284	
	1644	109	285	
	1643	110	286	Death of Joseph (Gen. 50: 22-26).
	1642		287	
	1641		288	
	1640		289	
	1639		290	
	1638		291	
	1637		292	
	1636		293	? Death of Levi.
The reign of Amenhotep IV followed by short reigns in Egypt.	1635		294	
	1634		295	
	1633		296	
	1632		297	
	1631		298	
	1630		299	
	1629		300	

NOTES.

EXPLANATIONS OF THE DATES

a B. C. 1628. Amenhotep IV reigned more than 17 years, and was succeeded by perhaps three weak kings, who vacillated between Amon and Aton. Then Harmhab, a general and a man of experience in public affairs, took the throne and ruled strongly for more than 34 years. Perhaps he should be counted as the first king of the nineteenth dynasty. He restored the Amon cult.

In Assyria Asshur-uballit had as lineal successors Bel-nirari, Budu-ilu, Ramman-nirari I. Their reigns were probably long, but the length is unknown. In Babylon the successors of Kuri-galzu included the kings Nazi-maruttash and Kadashman-turgu. After these, the Babylonian succession seems to me uncertain, and is partly blank, and the Assyrian succession is blank.

Foreign Dated Events.	B.C.	A. Mig.	Israelitish Dated Events.
About this time Harmhab of the nineteenth dynasty succeeds in Egypt. *a*	1628	301	
In Assyria the long reign of Asshur-uballit.	1627	302	
In Babylon the successor of Burna-buriash overthrown by Nazi-bugash. Asshur-uballit overthrows him and places on the throne "Kuri-galzu, the second," son of Burna-buriash.	1626	303	
	1625	304	
	1624	305	
	1623	306	
	1622	307	
	1621	308	
	1620	309	
	1619	310	
	1618	311	Israel in Egypt.
	1617	312	
	1616	313	
	1615	314	
	1614	315	
	1613	316	
	1612	317	
	1611	318	
	1610	319	
	1609	320	
	1608	321	
	1607	322	
	1606	323	
	1605	324	
	1604	325	

NOTES.

a A. Mig. 330. The accounts of the oppression speak of the great numbers of the Israelites in Egypt. At the exodus they make the number to be 600,000 adult men (Ex. 12: 37). This number is to be interpreted by the two census accounts (Num. 1 and 26). As the details are in even hundreds and thousands, clearly the enumeration is of regiments and companies rather than of individuals, and we naturally infer that few of the hundreds and thousands were full, and that many of them were far from full. That is, a strictly individual count would give a much smaller aggregate. The lowest estimate, however, cannot be less than many hundreds of thousands. As the Israelites were characteristically rural and pastoral in their occupations, and as they lived mingled with other peoples, the territory over which they spread must have been some thousands of square miles. They and their flocks had long distances to travel when they started from their homes, at the exodus. In forming our picture of what took place, we should not neglect these facts.

EXPLANATIONS OF THE DATES.

It is evident that the oppression began years after the death of Joseph, and years before the birth of Moses. Probably not early in the reign of Harmhab, and not violent during his reign.

The exodus occurred just at the close of the year 430 A. Mig. (Ex. 12: 40, 41, see Introduction 36*b*). Moses was then 80 years old (Ex. 7: 7). Hence the first year of his life was 351 A. Mig., and Aaron was born 3 years earlier. We infer that the law for slaying the male children was made within those three years.

Kohath died at the age of 133 (Ex. 6: 18). See notes at A. Mig. 213 and 28c.

Foreign Dated Events.	? B.C.	A. Mig.	Israelitish Dated Events.
	1603	326	
	1602	327	
	1601	328	
	1600	329	
	1599	330	? The oppression of Israel begins *a* (Ex. 1).
	1598	331	
	1597	332	
	1596	333	
Kings of the Kassite dynasty in Babylon.	1595	334	
	1594	335	
About this time Harmhab succeeded by Rameses I, and he, after 2 years, by Seti I.	1593	336	
	1592	337	
	1591	338	
	1590	339	
Palestine and the more distant regions, formerly subjugated by Thutmose I and Thutmose III, have become independent, and Seti and his son Rameses II have to reconquer them.	1589	340	
	1588	341	
	1587	342	
	1586	343	
	1585	344	
	1584	345	? Death of Kohath, the son of Levi.
	1583	346	
	1582	347	
	1581	348	Birth of Aaron (Ex. 7:7).
	1580	349	
	1579	350	? Law for destroying male infants (Ex. 1:15–22).

Notes.

a A. Mig. 351. Modern treatments are apt to ignore the biblical numerals, and crowd the events of the infancy of Moses into the reign of Rameses II.

The exploits of Moses as given in Josephus include many fanciful additions to the Bible story (*Ant.* II. ix–xi).

Israel continued to increase rapidly. Apparently the law for slaying the male infants fell into disuse.

Explanations of the Dates.

The exodus occurred just after the close of the year 430 A. Mig., so near to the close of the year that the difference is negligible (Ex. 12: 40, 41). The death of Moses occurred shortly before the year's close 40 years later. Moses was 80 years old at the beginning of the 40 years of the exodus, and 120 years old at their close (Ex. 7: 7; Deut. 31: 2, 34: 7).

THE TABLES

FOREIGN DATED EVENTS.	? B. C.	MOSES.	A. MIC.	ISRAELITISH DATED EVENTS.
	1578	1	351	Birth and infancy of Moses *a* (Ex. 1 : 1–2 : 10).
	1577	2	352	
	1576	3	353	
	1575	4	354	
	1574	5	355	
	1573	6	356	
	1572	7	357	
Kings of the Kassite dynasty in Babylonia.	1571	8	358	
	1570	9	359	
	1569	10	360	
	1568	11	361	
About this time begin the 67 years of Rameses II in Egypt.	1567	12	362	Israel in Egypt.
	1566	13	363	
	1565	14	364	
	1564	15	365	
	1563	16	366	
	1562	17	367	
	1561	18	368	
	1560	19	369	
	1559	20	370	
	1558	21	371	
	1557	22	372	
	1556	23	373	
	1555	24	374	
	1554	25	375	

Notes.

a A. Mig. 390. Jethro and his clan were Kenites by race (Jud. 1:16, 4:11; 1 Sam. 15:6). It is only in a geographical sense that they are called Midianite (Ex. 2:15, 16, 3:1, 4:19, 18:1; Num. 10:29).

Explanations of the Dates.

For the date when Moses went to Midian we accept Stephen's testimony (Acts 7:23, 30), "well nigh 40 years old."

It is correct to say that the biblical forties may supposably be general, but each forty is to be considered by itself. In the life of Moses the first 80 and the last 40 are given as exact numbers, while the division of the 80 into two forties is by its terms merely general.

Foreign Dated Events.	? B. C.	Moses.	A. Mig.	Israelitish Dated Events.
	1553	26	376	
	1552	27	377	
	1551	28	378	
	1550	29	379	
	1549	30	380	
	1548	31	381	
	1547	32	382	
	1546	33	383	
	1545	34	384	
	1544	35	385	
Kings of the Kassite dynasty in Babylon.	1543	36	386	
Rameses II in Egypt.	1542	37	387	Israel in Egypt.
	1541	38	388	
	1540	39	389	
	1539	40	390	Moses goes to Midian *a* (Ex. 2 : 11-22).
	1538	41	391	
	1537	42	392	
	1536	43	393	
	1535	44	394	
	1534	45	395	
	1533	46	396	
	1532	47	397	
	1531	48	398	
	1530	49	399	
	1529	50	400	

68 DATED EVENTS OF THE OLD TESTAMENT

NOTES.

EXPLANATIONS OF THE DATES.

Amram died at the age of 137 (Ex. 6: 20). See notes at A. Mig. 213, 280, 345.

THE TABLES

Foreign Dated Events.	? B. C.	Moses.	A. Mig.	Israelitish Dated Events.
	1528	51	401	
	1527	52	402	
	1526	53	403	
	1525	54	404	
	1524	55	405	
	1523	56	406	
	1522	57	407	
	1521	58	408	
	1520	59	409	
	1519	60	410	
Kings of the Kassite dynasty in Babylon.	1518	61	411	
Rameses II in Egypt.	1517	62	412	Israel in Egypt.
	1516	63	413	
	1515	64	414	
	1514	65	415	
	1513	66	416	? Death of Amram.
	1512	67	417	
	1511	68	418	
	1510	69	419	
	1509	70	420	
	1508	71	421	
	1507	72	422	
	1506	73	423	
	1505	74	424	
	1504	75	425	

NOTES.

a A. Mig. 430. Pharaoh's first rejection of Moses occurred after the harvest, and while the stubble (or the refuse of the threshing floors) remained in the fields (Ex. 5: 12). The seventh of the ten plagues was at a season such that the barley and the flax, but not the wheat and the spelt, were destroyed by the hail (Ex. 9: 31, 32). The tenth plague was after the beginning of Nisan. It follows that the narrated events covered several months, closing nearly with the close of the vernal year A. Mig. 430.

b A. Mig. 431. The Jethro division into thousands, hundreds, etc., was the census. It was made before the tent of meeting was finished (Ex. 38: 25-28), but officially promulgated the second year (Num. 1: 1-3 and 1: 18). "At that time" (Deut. 1: 9, 6).

EXPLANATIONS OF THE DATES.

A. Mig. 431, first month.
Day 10, Lamb taken (Ex. 12: 3).
    14, Lamb slain (12: 6, 18).
        Firstborn slain (12: 12–14).
    15, They start from their homes.
        ? Rameses to Succoth (12: 37).
        ? To Etham (13: 20).
        ? To Pi-hahiroth (14: 2).
        Crossing the Red Sea.
        3 days in the wilderness (15: 22).
        Marah (15: 23–26).
        Elim (15: 27).
Second month, 15th day, wilderness of Sin (16: 1).
Third month, 1st day, Sinai (19: 1).
x days, including 6 and 3 (24: 16, 19: 11).
40 days in mount (Ex. 24: 18; Deut. 9: 9, 11).
40 days of intercession (Deut. 9: 18, 25).
40 days in mount (Ex. 34: 28; Deut. 10: 10).

These events filled more than half the year. In the latter half occurred the making of the tabernacle, the ark, etc. (Ex. 25–39), the visit of Jethro, at "the mount of God" (Ex. 18), and the organization into thousands, hundreds, etc. *b* (Ex. 18: 21–25).

Foreign Dated Events.	? B.C.	Moses.	A. Mig.	Israelitish Dated Events.
	1503	76	426	
	1502	77	427	
About this time the 67 years of Rameses II close, and the reign of Merneptah begins.	1501	78	428	Moses at the burning bush, his return to Egypt, his message to Israel, his negotiations with Pharaoh, the ten plagues a (Ex. 3-11).
	1500	79	429	
	1499	80	430	
	1498	81	431	The exodus (Ex. 12-39). See opposite page.
	1497	82	432	First day, the tent of meeting set up (Ex. 40, especially 2, 17); the tent, altar, furniture and priests anointed (Ex. 40:9-16, cf. 29:7, 36; Lev. 8:10-12; Num. 7:1).
	1496	83	433	
	1495	84	434	First 7 days, the priests, tent, etc., set apart, Moses officiating day by day (Ex. 29:35-37; Lev. 8-10).
	1494	85	435	
	1493	86	436	First 12 days, offerings (Num. 7:1, 10, 12 . . . 78), beginning the day when the altar was anointed.
	1492	87	437	
Kings of the Kassite dynasty in Babylon.	1491	88	438	8th day, Aaron takes charge; fire on altar (Lev. 8-9, especially 8:33-35, 9:1; Ex. 29:35-37). Nadab and Abihu (Lev. 10).
	1490	89	439	
After a reign of more than 10 years, Merneptah is succeeded by three other kings, reigning briefly one after the other, and then there are "many years" of anarchy.	1489	90	440	The tribal offerings for this and the following 4 days continue as before.
	1488	91	441	14th day at evening, regular passover (Num. 9:1-5).
	1487	92	442	Second month, first day, census published. See note b. Various arrangements (Num. 1-8).
	1486	93	443	14th day, second passover (Num. 9). 20th day, the march begun (Num. 10). 3 days (10:33).
About this time, or perhaps much earlier (see Gen. Chaps. 21, 26, and Note b on A. Mig. 103), the original Philistines forcibly made their settlements on the coast. They were Greek pirates, but they married native women, and their descendants rapidly became Semiticized in language and civilization (see Deut. 2:23; Am. 9:7; Jer. 47:4).	1485	94	444	One month and more (Num. 11:19, 20, 21). Taberah, manna, Eldad and Medad, quails, the plague (Num. 10-11). 7 days and more, Miriam (Num. 12). 40 days at Kadesh (Num. 13:25). Season of grapes, figs, pomegranates (23), that is, about mid-year.
	1484	95	445	
	1483	96	446	
	1482	97	447	
	1481	98	448	The years of wandering begin (Num. 13-17); many days in Kadesh; 38 years from Kadesh to Zered (Deut. 1:46, 2:14).
	1480	99	449	
	1479	100	450	

Notes.

a Events of A. Mig. 471.

1st month: the command to advance (Josh. 1: 1–9); 6th day, spies in Jericho before sunset (2: 1–5); 7th to 9th days, the spies in the mountain country 3 days (2: 16, 22); 7th day, notice to move in 3 days (1: 11, 3: 2).

Conference with the two and a half tribes (1: 12–18).

9th day: from Shittim into line along the river (1: 11, 3: 2); "lodged there," "morrow" (3: 1, 5 cf. 4: 19).

The night by the river (*ibid.* and 3: 7). Return of the spies.

10th day: the crossing (4: 19).

The re-circumcision (5: 2–15).

14th and 15th days: passover (5: 10).

16th day: wave-sheaf? unleavened cakes and roast ears (5: 11–12; cf. Lev. 23: 11, 14).

7 days and more: Jericho (6: 1, 4, etc.).

Some weeks: the region north from Jericho; Ai (Josh. 7–8).

7th month? Ebal and Gerizim (8: 34–35; cf. Deut. 31: 10–13).

The Gibeonites (Josh. 9); battle of Gibeon and consequences (Josh. 10).

Explanations of the Dates.

Events of A. Mig. 470.

The march north from the Elanitic region (Deut. 2: 3; Num. 33: 36).

1st month: rendezvous at Kadesh, death of Miriam, water from the rock, message to Edom, march from Kadesh to Hor (Num. 20: 1–22).

5th month, 1st day: death of Aaron, 123 years old (Num. 20: 23–29, 33: 38–39).

30 days of mourning (20: 29).

Arad, march from Mount Hor, serpent of brass, Zered after 38 years (Num. 33: 40–41, 21: 1–12; Deut. 2: 14 and context).

Conquest of Sihon and Og (Num. 21; Deut. 2–3).

The encamping in the Jordan valley, Balaam, Beth-peor, second census, announcement of the succession of Joshua, war with Midian (Num. 22–31; Deut. 2–4).

First assignment of territory, that to the two and a half tribes (Num. 32; Deut. 3: 12–20); laws for land-division, cities of refuge, etc. (Num. 33: 50–36: 13).

11th month, 1st day: the first address in Deuteronomy, with the setting apart of three cities of refuge (Deut. 1: 3–4: 43; Num. 35: 14).

The remaining parts of Deuteronomy purport to be of about the same date.

Death of Moses and 30 days of mourning (Deut. 31–34; Num. 27: 12–23).

THE TABLES

Foreign Dated Events.	? B. C.	Moses.	A. Mig.	Israelitish Dated Events.
	1478	101	451	The middle part of the 40 years (about 37½ years of actual time) of the "wandering in the wilderness." Israel exists in the form of hundreds of small bands, in the regions both west and east of the eastern arm of the Red Sea, living the hard life of "shepherds in the wilderness" (Num. 14:33).
	1477	102	452	
	1476	103	453	
	1475	104	454	
	1474	105	455	
	1473	106	456	
	1472	107	457	
	1471	108	458	
	1470	109	459	
	1469	110	460	
Kings of the Kassite dynasty in Babylon.	1468	111	461	
	1467	112	462	
In Egypt, confusion, or, perhaps, the twentieth dynasty.	1466	113	463	
	1465	114	464	
	1464	115	465	
	1463	116	466	
	1462	117	467	
	1461	118	468	
	1460	119	469	Israel in the region of Mount Seir, the Red Sea and Ezion-geber (Deut. 2:1-3; Num. 33:35).
	1459	120	470	For events see opposite page.
	1458	Joshua: 1	471	For events see opposite page. *a*
	1457	2	472	? Battle of the waters of Merom (Josh. 11).
	1456	3	473	
	1455	4	474	
	1454	5	475	Second assignment of territory (Josh. 13-17). Caleb's 45 years minus 40 (Josh. 14:10).

NOTES.

a A. Mig. 476. The events are:
The locating of the Tent (Josh. 18:1ff).
The surveying of the land (3–9).
Casting lots in Shiloh (18:10–19:51).
Giving cities of refuge (20).
Cities for the priests (21).
Return of the 40,000 (22).
Considerations of weather and business indicate that the affair began about the time of the autumnal feast. Within a few weeks the citizens were probably in their new homes, engaged in agricultural operations for the coming year.

b A. Mig. 479. The earlier subjugation of the same regions (Josh. 10) seems not to have been sufficiently thorough.

c A. Mig. 495. Josephus says (*Ant.* V, i, 28, 29) that the administration of Joshua lasted 25 years. Joshua was associated with Moses from the beginning, being younger than Moses, though perhaps not much younger (Ex. 33:11, 17:9, 24:13, etc). Such phrases as "long time," "old and well stricken in years" (Josh. 11:18, 13:1) are used for the times before the second distribution of territory, as well as "many days" for the times after (Josh. 23:1). Eight years seems to me a more probable limit than twenty-five.

EXPLANATIONS OF THE DATES.

For reasons given on the following pages these events must be placed as compactly as possible. The first assignment of territory was that by Moses, east of the Jordan (Num. 32), to two and a half tribes. The second, to Judah, Ephraim and Manasseh (Josh. 13-17), is dated (14:10) 45 years after the sending of the spies from Kadesh. This was $38\frac{1}{2}$ years before the accession of Joshua, but is presumably counted as an even 40 years, making the date the 5th year of Joshua rather than the 6th or 7th. The third assignment, to the remaining 7 tribes, and partly of territory that had already been given to Judah and Joseph, must have come soon after. Josephus (*Ant.* V, i, 19) combines the second and third, giving the date as the 5th year of Joshua.

THE TABLES

FOREIGN DATED EVENTS.	? B. C.	JOSHUA.	A. MIG.	ISRAELITISH DATED EVENTS.
	1453	6	476	? Setting up the tent at Shiloh, *a* and the third assignment of territory (Josh. 18–21).
About this time the 31 years of Rameses III of the twentieth dynasty in Egypt.	1452	7	477	? Joshua's first convocation (Josh. 23).
	1451	?	478	? Joshua's second convocation (Josh. 24).
	1450		479	? Death of Joshua (Josh. 24: 29–30).
	1449		480	? Further conquests, *b* Judah and Caleb at the front (Jud. 1: 1–20; Josh. 15: 14–19).
	1448		481	
	1447		482	
	1446		483	
	1445		484	
	1444		485	
	1443		486	
Kings of the Kassite dynasty in Babylon.	1442		487	
	1441		488	? Oppression of Cushan-rishathaim.
	1440		489	
	1439		490	
	1438		491	
	1437		492	
	1436		493	
	1435		494	
	1434		495	Death of Joshua, according to Josephus. *c*

SECOND TABLE

JOSHUA TO SOLOMON

THE SECOND CHRONOLOGICAL PERIOD

The formative historical period closes with the establishment of Israel in the promised land, and for that reason we have extended the era of the migration of Abraham so as to make it include the exploits of Joshua. The transition of chronological method, however, is at the beginning of Joshua's career (unless one places it 40 years earlier, at the opening of the exodus period), so that for some purposes there is an overlap of the two periods. For this new period note three introductory points.

The Biblical Forties.—The number of periods of forty years each for the history between Moses and Solomon is so large as to be noticeable. It is well enough to say that the 40 in these cases is a round number, and may be far from exact, but one ought to look at each instance by itself. The 40 years of the exodus are defined as opening and closing so near the end of the year that the inexactness is a negligible quantity. The 40 years of king David are defined to be $40\frac{1}{2}$ years (2 Sam. 5: 4-5), and are treated chronologically, as we shall see, as 41 years. The respective forties of Solomon, of Saul, of Eli, of the Philistines (1 Ki. 11:42; Acts 13:21; 1 Sam. 4:18; Jud. 13:1) are undefined. There remain the four instances in which the formula is used, "the land had rest 40 years" (Jud. 3:11, 30, 5:31, 8:28). The natural suggestion is that we have here a section of the narrative in which the chronology is kept in continuous periods of 40 years, the other numbers used being included in the forties. This suggestion is followed in the tables, its correctness being confirmed by the test of practical use (see Introduction 35).

The International Situation at the Time of the Conquest.—In Joshua 13-17 we have an account of the giving of territory to two and a half tribes west of the Jordan. Two and a half tribes have previously received their territory east of the Jordan. The suggestion is that the remaining seven tribes will be provided for on the same scale, and largely from land yet to be conquered. Instead of this, when the final distribution comes (Josh. 18-21), the scale is vastly reduced, and the territory of three of the seven tribes is largely carved out of that which had been previously assigned. This suggests the arising of a condition of things in which the main movement of conquest has been suddenly and unexpectedly arrested. I suppose that the records of Rameses III of Egypt give us two great facts that have a bearing on this matter.

The first of these facts is this. He says that the closing time of the nineteenth dynasty was a time of lawlessness and bad conditions in Egypt, and that it was followed by an interim of "many years" in which things were as bad as possible. He mentions a Syrian named Arsu as having things all his own way. Out of this, in the second year before the reign of Rameses began, he and his father rescued Egypt. If the confusion in Egypt lasted into the years when Joshua was overrunning Canaan, and if then a strong government was established in Egypt, obviously Israel would be compelled to take into account the change thus made.

The other fact is the great invasion of the whole region by hordes from the north. As long previously as the reign of Merneptah, Egypt was at war with peoples bearing Greek names, peoples of northern Africa and their allies from other coasts. Of these, the Philistines and others had effected settlements on the east Mediterranean coast. There came a time when in a concerted movement from all Greek regions numberless hordes poured south, by land and by sea, to plunder and occupy Egypt and the countries on the way. The crisis came in the eighth year of Rameses III. He claims to have defeated the hordes by land in southern Palestine, and to have defeated them by sea.

If the exodus occurred under Merneptah then Israel had relations of some kind with these events narrated by Rameses III. Egypt had held dominion, and still claimed dominion over Canaan; are Joshua's Israelites the hordes by land whom Rameses describes? Or did Israel make common cause with the other Palestinian peoples and with Egypt against the northern hordes? This is not the place to discuss the part that Israel took, but obviously it cannot have been that of an inactive spectator.

I have adjusted the table of events on the theory that Joshua's great movement of conquest was brought to an end by the establishment of the Egyptian twentieth dynasty and the events that followed.

Chronological Problems of David's Reign.—These are of peculiar importance, and have been phenomenally neglected.

Our most original sources of information here are the second book of Samuel and the first chapter of Kings. In 1 Chronicles the statements of Samuel and Kings are repeated in part and supplemented. These sources, either in the specific statements they make or through the nature of the events, give the data for a substantially complete chronology, but the successive narratives in them are not arranged in chronological order. In 2 Samuel the last four chapters are made up of six short pieces dealing with events of different dates. The eighth chapter is a summary of events, some of the details of which are repeated in Chapters 10–12. The events of the sixth and seventh chapters belong, in time, after most of those of chapters 8–12. These facts do not indicate incompetence on the part of the writer or writers, but rather that the book is a collection of memoranda, not digested into a continuous story. The writer in Chronicles follows the order of Samuel only in part, but makes no attempt to establish an order of time for the several narratives.

Unfortunately, Josephus ignored all this. He assumes that the events in 2 Samuel 24 are later than the rebellions of Absalom and Sheba spoken of in the preceding chapters, and that therefore the events mentioned in 1 Chronicles after the twenty-first chapter are still later. In his consequent distorted and impossible presentation of the reign of David he has been generally followed. The scholars of the newer tradition, instead of correcting his blunder, make it the basis of their inference that our accounts of David are largely unhistorical. By the usual biblical way of counting, David's reign of 40 years and 6 months (2 Sam. 5: 4–5) would be spoken of as 41 years. At the close of his fortieth year he had one year yet to reign.

The Chronicler (1 Chron. 21 and 22: 1) regards the purchase of Ornan's threshing floor as the determining of the site for the temple, and proceeds to give details as to David's preparations for the temple and its worship. Some of the details are in fragmentary shape, but they are framed together by headings into a systematic whole (1 Chron. 22: 1–29: 22a). The preparations include the making of Solomon king, and the holding of a great public assembly (1 Chron. 23: 1 and 28: 1–29: 22a), and the account terminates with the sacrificial feast at the close of the assembly (29: 22a). It is immediately followed by a brief account (1 Chron. 29: 22b–24, which ought to be printed as a paragraph separate from what precedes) of Solomon's being made king a second time. Nearly the entire phraseology of this paragraph is repeated from the first chapter of 1 Kings, and the paragraph is evidently an epitome of that chapter. Solomon's being made king the second time was in connection with Adonijah's attempt to take the kingdom. His being made king the first time was an earlier affair, and something had occurred between the two to render the second affair necessary.

The Chronicler dates some of these temple preparations, and by inference dates them generally, in the fortieth year of David (1 Chron. 26: 31). The natural suggestion is that the 9 months and 20 days of the census (2 Sam. 24: 8) began in David's 39th year, and closed at the wheat threshing season (1 Chron. 21: 20) in the 40th year, and that the great public assembly was at the close of the 40th year.

Absalom's rebellion broke out just after the close of David's 40th year (2 Sam. 15: 7), David's flight occurring in his 41st year in the time of bruised corn, shortly before the harvest (2 Sam. 17: 19, 28). There was time after that in that year for the operations against Absalom and Sheba, the schemes of Adonijah, and the first events of the reign of Solomon.

These facts, with the numerical data found in 2 Samuel, give us the chronology of the last 12 years of David's reign, beginning with the thirtieth. The earlier 21 years of his reign over all Israel naturally divide themselves into two periods, a period of strenuous fighting and a period of rest. As mention is made of six campaigns against the Philistines and five or more against the eastern and northern peoples (see the tables), we may conjecturally assign about 13 years to the fighting period, and about 8 years to the rest period.

David's great sin in the matter of Uriah occurred near the close of the fighting period.

The bringing of the ark to Jerusalem (2 Sam. 6; 1 Chron. 13, 15, 16) occurred after the fighting period, when David's conquests were substantially complete. Not till then could he have assembled Israel "from the Shihor of Egypt even unto the entrance of Hamath" (1 Chron. 13: 5). The Chronicler's statement that the removal of the ark occurred, not soon after David's capture of Jerusalem, but a good many years later, after David's victories in war, after his repentance for his great sin, when the country had become secure and prosperous and Jerusalem had become magnificent, is confirmed by the details as given in both Samuel and Chronicles. Later came the great promise (2 Sam. 7; 1 Chron. 17), when Jehovah had given David rest from all his enemies round about (2 Sam. 7: 1).

We have already seen that this view of the chronology brings the events of the external history into an orderly sequence quite in contrast with the violently improbable order involved in the Josephan cast of the events. While David was king in Hebron both he and Ishbosheth probably accepted the suzerainty of the Philistines. When David was made king of Israel of course the Philistines objected. Having repulsed them in two successive campaigns, David was too wise a general not to carry the war into the enemy's country, and in course of time he took the reins away from the Philistines (2 Sam. 8: 1), and held them himself. His other conquests followed, and his sin and his repentance, and his interest in the building of a temple, and his fondness for Solomon. It is no wonder that dissatisfaction arose over the prominence thus given to Jerusalem, and no wonder that there came to be a legitimist party which preferred the succession of elder sons of David to that of Solomon. All these things follow in consecutive order when we once get the correct point of view.

The same is true of the personal experience of David. Following the Josephan theory the ethical history of David is a series of contradictions; it becomes an intelligible continuity when we arrange it on the line of the biblical time data. Up to the time of the death of Samuel David's conduct is not merely exemplary, but fine. Then he begins to deteriorate. He plans to avenge himself on Nabal. He begins the practice of marrying wives for the sake of political influence. In the land of the Philistines he practices horrible and unjust cruelties. He gets himself into a position where he must choose between faithlessness to Israel and treachery to Achish, his benefactor, and escapes from it only through his having such a reputation that the Philistine lords do not trust him. In these and the following events he maintains many of the virtues that belong to a great leader, but in other directions he continues to deteriorate. A time comes when he ceases from active military service (2 Sam. 21: 17), though he is not ashamed to take credit for the exploits which others have wrought in his service (2 Sam. 12: 27–29). He gives himself more and more to luxury and self-indulgence. At length this culminates in the Uriah sin, with all the aggravations that mark it as a peculiarly ungrateful, atrocious, foolish, mean, low-down piece of conduct. Other kings, ancient and modern, have done dirtier deeds, but, in view of David's moral capabilities, it was for him a plunge into the lowest depths. Then came his repentance, which was sincere and thorough, but which did not relieve him from the entanglements of his bad past. He became mindful of the obligations of friendship, and took care of Mephibosheth. He became mindful of religious obligations, and made provision for the ark and the sanctuary. But he could not get rid of Joab, his colleague in crime. He could not prevent the feuds that arose among the children of his polygamous marriages. He could not prevent Amnon and Absalom and Adonijah from following the bad example he had set them. Ahithophel was as treacherous with him as he himself had been with Uriah. The climax came early in his forty-first year, when his splendid demonstration for Solomon and the temple was presently followed by the simultaneous outburst everywhere of the Absalom rebellion. David bore up bravely as long as the contests with Absalom and Sheba continued, and then became a broken old man. It was with difficulty that Nathan and Bathsheba aroused in him a flash of his old-time spirit, for placing Solomon on the throne instead of Adonijah.

A true chronology brings a like continuity into the religious history of the period. In the times of his deterioration David had never forgotten Jehovah, but he had become careless in regard to the national religion. As his sons became men, he made priests of them (2 Sam. 8: 18). After his repentance he turned his attention to the ark, but at first without due care. It was necessary for Jehovah to rebuke him through the death of Uzza, in order to lead him to take the pains requisite to serve as Jehovah required to be served. After that we have no account of any irregularities on David's part.

Notes.

a A. T. J. stands for *Anno Transitus Jordanis*, the year when Israel crossed the Jordan under Joshua.

b The years of Joshua and of others from this point are those of their term of leadership, not as heretofore of the years of their life. This is an item in the change of chronological method which here marks a change of era.

c B. C. 1452. The notable wars mentioned by Rameses III are those with the Lybians in his fifth year, with the northern hordes in his eighth year, with the Lybians in his eleventh year, and in Syria, believed to have been soon after the last.

d A. T. J. 18. Who was Cushan-rishathaim? Josephus describes him as Chusarth, king of the Assyrians (*Ant.* V, iii, 2). As good a guess as any is that he was Rameses III.

Explanations of the Dates.

Most of the dates on this page are inferential, depending more or less on a theory of the Egyptian synchronisms.

For the events of the time of Joshua see at A. Mig. 470–478.

The margin of supposable variation is pretty wide for the dates on this page. The 8 years of Cushan-rishathaim might be placed in some other part of the 40 years.

Josephus assigns 25 years to Joshua, and speaks of an "anarchy" of 18 years following (*Ant.* V, i, 29 and VI, v, 4. See at A T. J. 229). Possibly he would be correct if he included the 18 in the 25.

THE TABLES

Foreign Dated Events.	? B. C.	Joshua. b	A. T. J. a	Israelitish Dated Events.
	1458	1	1	The conquest, south (Josh. 1-10).
	1457	2	2	? The conquest, north and summary (Josh. 11-12).
	1456	3	3	
	1455	4	4	
	1454	5	5	Territory to Judah, Ephraim, Manasseh (Josh. 13-17).
	1453	6	6	? The tent placed; final division of territory (Josh. 18-22).
? About this time the accession of Rameses III, the second king of the twentieth dynasty. c	1452	7	7	? Convocation (Josh. 23).
	1451	?	8	? Shechem convocation, and death of Joshua (Josh. 24).
	1450		9	? Further conquests (Jud. 1; Josh. 15 : 14-19).
	1449		10	
Kings of the Kassite dynasty in Babylon.	1448		11	
	1447		12	
	1446		13	
? About this time Rameses defeats the hordes from the north.	1445	Cushan-rishathaim.	14	
	1444		15	
	1443		16	
? About this time the second Lybian war of Rameses.	1442		17	
? About this time Rameses invades Syria.	1441	1	18	? Oppression by Cushan-rishathaim d (Jud. 3 : 7-11).
	1440	2	19	
	1439	3	20	
	1438	4	21	
	1437	5	22	
	1436	6	23	
	1435	7	24	
	1434	8	25	[Death of Joshua, according to Josephus.]

Notes.

a A. T. J. 26. See Explanations and Notes at A. T. J. 25 and 229.

b A. T. J. 26. Othniel was Caleb's son-in-law, distinguished in the wars that followed the death of Joshua (Jud. 1: 10–15; Josh. 15: 13–20). The probabilities concerning his age fit the time limits here assigned.

c A. T. J. 37. The policy of exterminating the Canaanites was bound up with the divine promise in the matter. The revocation of the promise (Jud. 2: 1–5) implies a change from that time in the policy. Henceforth the Canaanites were under the same law with other conquered nations (Deut. 20: 11–15), subject to *mas*, that is, to compulsory service (cf. Ex. 1: 11), instead of being made an exception to the law (Deut. 20: 15–18). The narratives say that this changed policy was adopted (Josh. 16: 10, 17: 13; Jud. 1: 28, 30, 33, 35).

Explanations of the Dates.

The distribution of the events is open to difference of opinion. "The land had rest 40 years" is a phrase in which the count is to the final terminus only (Int. 19*d*), Josephus to the contrary notwithstanding (*Ant.* V, iii, 3). The meaning is that there are no further events which the writer will put on record, up to the close of the forty-year period then current.

The one fixed fact is that the 8 years of Cushan-rishathaim belong somewhere between the death of Joshua and the close of the 40 years. If we followed Josephus in regarding Cushan-rishathaim as Assyrian (Note *d*, A. T. J. 18), we might place his 8 years later in the 40.

In the Leshem narrative a grandson of Moses appears as a young man (Jud. 18: 30, 3, 15 and 17: 7). The incident was long enough before the Benjamite war to justify the expression "from Dan even to Beersheba" in the narrative, and that war was before the death of Phinehas (Jud. 20: 1, 28).

THE TABLES

Foreign Dated Events.	?B.C.	A.T.J.	Israelitish Dated Events.
	1433	26	The "anarchy" of Josephus? *a*
	1432	27	Othniel, *b* deliverer and judge for an unknown length of time, till the close of the period of 40 years (Jud. 3:7-11).
	1431	28	
	1430	29	
	1429	30	
	1428	31	
	1427	32	
	1426	33	
	1425	34	
Rameses III in Egypt.	1424	35	
Kings of the Kassite dynasty in Babylon.	1423	36	
	1422	37	? The Angel at Bochim *c* (Jud. 2:1-5). ? The adoption of the *mas* policy.
	1421	38	
	1420	39	
	1419	40	FIRST FORTY-YEAR PERIOD ENDS (Jud. 3:11).
	1418	41	
	1417	42	
	1416	43	? Leshem captured and named Dan (Josh. 19:47; Jud. 17-18).
	1415	44	
	1414	45	
	1413	46	
	1412	47	
	1411	48	
	1410	49	
	1409	50	

Notes.

a B. C. 1396. Shagashalti-buriash reigned, in round numbers, 800 years before Nabonidus, B. C. 555–539. That is, about B. C. 1345 Assyrian, or B. C. 1396 in these tables (see Introduction 26*b*, Third, and note at B. C. 1157).

b A. T. J. 64. Scattered through the Pentateuch and Joshua are allusions and items that presuppose events later than the death of Moses or of Joshua. Few or none of them presuppose anything later than the lifetime of Phinehas. On the hypothesis that a contemporary of Phinehas was the literary executor of Moses, there is very little need of the additional hypothesis of later changes, in order to account for all the phenomena.

Explanations of the Dates.

The war with Benjamin occurred after the establishment of Dan as the northern limit of Israel (Jud. 20: 1), and before the death of Phinehas, the grandson of Aaron (Jud. 20: 28). It left Israel demoralized. For some generations the Benjamites became especially cousins of Ephraim (Jud. 21).

The oppression by Eglon was made possible through the demoralizing effects of the war with Benjamin.

Phinehas (Num. 25: 7, 11, 31: 6; Psa. 106: 30; Josh. 22), though prominent before the death of Moses, was perhaps then a very young man. He may have survived Moses by 60 or more years without having lived to an extraordinary age.

THE TABLES

Foreign Dated Events.	? B.C.		A.T.J.	Israelitish Dated Events.
	1408		51	? Benjamite civil war (Jud. 19–21; Jos. *Ant.* V, ii, 8–12).
	1407		52	
	1406		53	
	1405		54	
	1404		55	
	1403		56	
	1402	EGLON OF MOAB.	57	
	1401		58	
	1400		59	
	1399		60	
From about this date materials for continuous Egyptian history are lacking for a long time.	1398		61	
	1397	1	62	? Beginning of the 18 years of the oppression by Eglon (Jud. 3 : 12–30, 10 : 11–12).
About this time, but with a wide margin for difference, Shagashaltiburiash, king of Babylon. *a*	1396	2	63	
	1395	3	64	? Latest hexateuchal events *b* (Josh. 24 : 29–33; Jud. 1, 2 : 6–9).
	1394	4	65	? The hexateuch completed.
	1393	5	66	? Death of Phinehas.
	1392	6	67	
	1391	7	68	
	1390	8	69	
	1389	9	70	
	1388	10	71	
	1387	11	72	
	1386	12	73	
	1385	13	74	
	1384	14	75	

Notes.

a A. T. J. 79. Ehud was a man of Benjamin (Jud. 3: 15), but he "blew a trumpet in the hill country of Ephraim" to raise his forces. Doubtless he was half Ephraimite, a son of one of the marriages of the girls seized by Benjamin at Shiloh (Jud. 21: 23). Both in paying tribute and in raising forces (Jud. 3: 15, 27-30) he acted as representative of Israel as a whole.

b B. C. 1375. See note at B. C. 1329.

Explanations of the Dates.

Doubtless the Moabite oppressor was at the head of a confederacy including the Ammonites and other peoples; but even so Israel, normally, would be too strong for him. It must be that he took advantage of the demoralization caused by the war against Benjamin. We must place the 18 years (Jud. 3: 14) of the oppression early enough for this, and late enough for Ehud to have grown up as one of the sons of the Ephraimite mothers.

The exact place of the 20 years of Jabin (Jud. 4: 3) in the third forty-year period (Jud. 5: 31) can only be conjectured.

THE TABLES

FOREIGN DATED EVENTS.	? B. C.	EGLON.	A. T. J.	ISRAELITISH DATED EVENTS.
	1383	15	76	
	1382	16	77	
	1381	17	78	
	1380	18	79	? *Ehud* of Benjamin deliverer. *a*
	1379		80	END OF SECOND 40-YEAR PERIOD (Jud. 3:30).
	1378		81	
	1377		82	
	1376		83	
About this time Shalmanezer I king in Assyria. *b*	1375		84	
	1374		85	
Kings of the Kassite dynasty in Babylon.	1373		86	
	1372	JABIN.	87	
	1371		88	
	1370	1	89	? Oppression by Jabin (Jud. 4-5).
	1369	2	90	
	1368	3	91	
	1367	4	92	
	1366	5	93	
	1365	6	94	
	1364	7	95	
	1363	8	96	
	1362	9	97	
	1361	10	98	
	1360	11	99	
	1359	12	100	

NOTES.

a A. T. J. 108. In Deborah's song the singer says, addressing Ephraim: "After thee [came down] Benjamin, among thy peoples." This was accurately the status of Benjamin, say two generations after the civil war closed with the marriage of the Benjamite warriors with the girls taken at Shiloh (Jud. 5:14, Jud. 21).

EXPLANATIONS OF THE DATES.

Concerning this first Philistine oppression we are able to gather a few facts. In Judges 10:11 a Philistine oppression is mentioned as following an Ammonite oppression. The latter may naturally be that of Eglon. Shamgar appears in Judges and Josephus (Jud. 3:31, 5:6; Jos. *Ant.* V, iv, 3). He is the contemporary of Jael and Deborah. There was a Philistine oppression contemporary with that of Jabin, and Shamgar, probably of Judah, was the deliverer. The Philistines pursued the same tactics as later, in Saul's time, disarming the Israelites (Jud. 5:8, 3:31; cf. 1 Sam. 13:19ff). Necessarily the Philistine yoke lay heaviest on the southern tribes, and this accounts for the absence of Judah and Simeon from Deborah's roll-call of the tribes

THE TABLES

Foreign Dated Events.	? B.C.	Jabin.	A.T.J.	Israelitish Dated Events.
	1358	13	101	
	1357	14	102	
	1356	15	103	
	1355	16	104	
	1354	17	105	
	1353	18	106	? Oppression by Philistines (Jud. 3:31).
	1352	19	107	
	1351	20	108	? *Shamgar* of Judah (?). ? *Deborah* of Ephraim. *a* ? *Barak* of Naphtali.
	1350		109	
	1349		110	
Kings of the Kassite dynasty in Babylon.	1348		111	
Shalmanezer I in Assyria.	1347		112	
	1346		113	
	1345		114	
	1344		115	
	1343		116	
	1342		117	
	1341		118	
	1340		119	
	1339		120	END OF THIRD FORTY YEARS (Jud. 5:31).
	1338		121	
	1337		122	
	1336		123	
	1335		124	
	1334		125	

NOTES.

a B. C. 1329. Sennacherib says that he brought back the seal in B. C. 689, after 600 years. This gives about B. C. 1288 (Assyrian) as the date when Tukulti-ninip went to Babylon with the seal. The Babylonian chronicle says (see *Records of the Past*, new series, V, 111) that he governed at Babylon 7 years, and was then displaced by Ramman-nadin-ahhi. This reign of 7 years is not recognized in the Babylonian list of kings. A king whose name is lost began a reign of 17 years in B. C. 1271 (Assyrian). This can be no other than Ramman-nadin-ahhi. His unknown predecessor is credited in the list with 26 years, and the last 7 of these must be the 7 years of Tukulti-ninip—beginning B. C. 1278 Assyrian, that is, B. C. 1329 in these tables.

Here a difficulty emerges. Tukulti-ninip was son to Shalmanezer I, who speaks of himself as son of Ramman-nirari I, the son of Budu-ilu (see note at B. C. 1628). Ramman-nirari was great-grandson to Asshur-uballit, the contemporary of Burna-buriash, whom these tables date about B. C. 1650. From B. C. 1650 to 1329 is too long an interval for this short succession of Assyrian kings.

The solution may lie in the hypothesis that Ramman-nirari was Shalmanezer's father only in the sense of being his ancestor or predecessor; like Asshur-uballit, whom Shalmanezer also calls his father (see note at B. C. 1157, also *Records of the Past*, new series II, 206). This hypothesis is thoroughly consistent with the Babylonian data of the period.

EXPLANATIONS OF THE DATES.

The oppression by the Midianites lasted 7 years (6:1), and the impression made by the narrative is that it came early in the forty-year period, leaving a longer time for the administration of Gideon than was had by most of the judges.

THE TABLES

Foreign Dated Events.	? B.C.		A.T.J.	Israelitish Dated Events.
	1333		126	
	1332		127	
	1331	MIDIANITES.	128	
	1330		129	
About this time Tukulti-ninip *a* of Assyria takes a seal to Babylon and governs there 7 years. His successor in Babylon is Ramman-nadin-ahhi, who reigns 17 years.	1329	1	130	? Oppression by the Midianites (Jud. 6-8).
	1328	2	131	
	1327	3	132	
	1326	4	133	
	1325	5	134	
	1324	6	135	
	1323	7	136	? *Gideon* of West Manasseh.
	1322		137	
	1321		138	
	1320		139	
	1319		140	
	1318		141	
At about this time Tukulti-ninip succeeded in Assyria by Asshur-natsir-pal.	1317		142	
	1316		143	
	1315		144	
	1314		145	
	1313		146	
	1312		147	
	1311		148	
	1310		149	
	1309		150	

Notes.

a B. C. 1305. The names and years of this and the eleven following Babylonian kings are taken from the list. The twelve reigns cover just 100 years.

b A. T. J. 160. Before Gideon the judges were raised up when needed, and there seem to have been intervals when Israel had no judge. Under Gideon a change to hereditary government was proposed (Jud. 8: 22–23). He refused, but an actual change of constitution then came in, the judges from that time directly succeeding one another. With this change the chronological method changes, the dates being henceforth given in terms of the years of the ruling judge, and no longer in terms of 40 years.

c A. T. J. 161. The title given to Abimelech is peculiar, but notice that it is national, no matter how local may be the recorded events of his career.

Explanations of the Dates.

The 40 years of Judges 8: 28, unlike the three preceding forties, connects itself with a particular event, the death of Gideon. Doubtless the 3 years of Abimelech (Jud. 9: 22) are counted from the close of the 40 years, whether the death of Gideon occurred exactly at that date or not.

Tola's 23 years (Jud. 10: 2).

THE TABLES

Foreign Dated Events.	P. B. C.		A. T. J.	Israelitish Dated Events.
	1308		151	
	1307		152	
	1306		153	
The first year of Kadashman-buriash *a* of Babylon.	1305		154	
	1304		155	
The first of the 6 years of Is-am-me . . . . ti of Babylon.	1303		156	
	1302		157	
	1301		158	
	1300		159	
	1299		160	END OF 4TH FORTY YEARS *b* (Jud. 8:28).
	1298	1	161	*Abimelech*, captain of Israel *c* (Jud. 9).
The first of the 13 years of Shagashalti-shuriash of Babylon.	1297	2	162	
	1296	3	163	
	1295	1	164	*Tola*, judge (Jud. 10:1-2), of Issachar, dwelling in Ephraim.
	1294	2	165	
	1293	3	166	
	1292	4	167	
	1291	5	168	
	1290	6	169	
	1289	7	170	
	1288	8	171	
	1287	9	172	
	1286	10	173	
	1285	11	174	
The first of the 8 years of Bibé of Babylon.	1284	12	175	

NOTES.

a A. T. J. 180. Properly speaking, we have no account at all of Samson's term as judge, but only of his wild youth before he became judge, and of the last few months of his life, when he relapsed into follies. His administration, however, judging by its apparent results, was a worthy one.

EXPLANATIONS OF THE DATES.

The story of Samson (Jud. 13–16) is out of chronological order, like the two stories that follow it (Jud. 17–18, 19–21). A Philistine oppression had begun before he was born, and was active before he became judge (Jud. 13: 5, 15: 11), but he seems to have taught the Philistines to keep on their own side of the border (Jud. 16), thus fulfilling the promise that he should begin to save Israel from them. Is this state of things mentioned elsewhere in the narrative?

It is by many identified with the times of Eli, but that is a hopeless misfit. It is rather the second Philistine oppression, which is mentioned between the account of Jair and that of the Ammonite oppression of Jephthah's time, and is distinguished from an earlier oppression, which must be that of Shamgar (Jud. 10: 7, 11). This fixes the 20 years of Samson's judging Israel (Jud. 15: 20, 16: 31) as next after the 22 years of Jair, and the probable date of his birth as some years before the accession of Jair.

THE TABLES

Foreign Dated Events.	? B. C.	Tola.	A. T. J.	Israelitish Dated Events.
	1283	13	176	? A second Philistine oppression begins (Jud. 10:7).
	1282	14	177	
	1281	15	178	
	1280	16	179	
	1279	17	180	? Birth of Samson *a* (Jud. 13).
	1278	18	181	
	1277	19	182	
The first of the 1½ years of Bel-shum-iddina of Babylon.	1276	20	183	
	1275	21	184	
? The close of the 1½ years of Kadashman-hharbe of Babylon.	1274	22	185	
The first of the 6 years of Ramman-shum-iddina of Babylon.	1273	23	186	
	1272	1	187	*Jair*, judge, a Gileadite of Manasseh (Jud. 10:3-5).
	1271	2	188	
	1270	3	189	
	1269	4	190	
	1268	5	191	
The first of the 30 years of Ramman-shum-utsur of Babylon. The contemporary kings of Assyria were Bel-Kudur-utsur and Ninip-pilezer (*Rec. of Past*, new series, IV, 29).	1267	6	192	
	1266	7	193	
	1265	8	194	
	1264	9	195	
	1263	10	196	
	1262	11	197	
	1261	12	198	
	1260	13	199	
	1259	14	200	

Notes.	Explanations of the Dates.
	See preceding pages.

THE TABLES

Foreign Dated Events.	? B.C.	Jair.	A.T.J.	Israelitish Dated Events.
	1258	15	201	
	1257	16	202	
	1256	17	203	
	1255	18	204	
	1254	19	205	
	1253	20	206	
	1252	21	207	? Samson's wild youth (Jud. 14–15).
	1251	22	208	
	1250	1	209	*Samson*, of the tribe of Dan, judge (Jud. 13–16).
	1249	2	210	
	1248	3	211	
	1247	4	212	
	1246	5	213	
	1245	6	214	
	1244	7	215	
? Perhaps Asshur-nirari and his son Nebo-dan in Assyria.	1243	8	216	
	1242	9	217	
	1241	10	218	
	1240	11	219	
	1239	12	220	
	1238	13	221	
The first of the 15 years of Meli-shihu of Babylon.	1237	14	222	
	1236	15	223	
	1235	16	224	
	1234	17	225	

NOTES.

a A. T. J. 229. "After the death of Joshua, for 18 years in all, the multitude had no settled form of government, but were an anarchy, after which they returned to their former polity . . . judged by . . . the best and most courageous warrior" (Jos. *Ant.* VI, v, 4). "Anarchy" here is not necessarily confusion; it may be merely the absence of centralized control. Presumably there is a traditional basis of some sort for this statement concerning 18 years. There is no room for an additional 18 years early in the history. If they belong there, they must either be included in the 25 years which Josephus assigns to Joshua (see at A. T. J 25 and Explanations), or must include the 8 years of Cushan-rishathaim, or both. I suspect, however, that the tradition was to the effect that there was a centralized government of some sort in Israel from Joshua to the monarchy, except for 18 years, and that the 18 years intended were those of the Ammonite oppression.

EXPLANATIONS OF THE DATES.

For the times of the successive judges, the times after Gideon, the length of an oppression in years is given only here and in Judges 13: 1. Presumably these numerals are given for their chronological value, and are to be counted as a part of the total. The narrative connects the 18 with the interval between the death of Jair and the accession of Jephthah. The 18 years of the oppression were followed by the 6 years of Jephthah (Jud. 12: 7).

Jephthah's round number 300 (Jud. 11: 26) would be very marked if we counted the 80 of Judges 3: 30 as excluding the 40 of Jud. 3: 11. By that way of counting, it was 287 years from Israel's conquest of Sihon to the first year of Jephthah. Counting the other way it is 247 years, and one may infer that Jephthah had in mind the date when Ammon lost the region to the Amorites from whom Israel took it.

THE TABLES

Foreign Dated Events.	?B.C.	Samson.	A.T.J.	Israelitish Dated Events.
? Asshur-daan I in Assyria. His reign may have begun earlier.	1233	18	226	
	1232	19	227	
	1231	20	228	Samson's foolish last deeds (Jud. 16).
	1230	1	229	Oppression by the Ammonites *a* (Jud. 10:7-18).
	1229	2	230	
	1228	3	231	
	1227	4	232	
	1226	5	233	
	1225	6	234	
	1224	7	235	
	1223	8	236	
The first of the 13 years of Marduk-pal-iddina of Babylon.	1222	9	237	
	1221	10	238	
	1220	11	239	
	1219	12	240	
	1218	13	241	
	1217	14	242	
	1216	15	243	
	1215	16	244	
	1214	17	245	
	1213	18	246	
	1212	1	247	*Jephthah*, of Gilead, judge (Jud. 11: 1-12:7). 300 years (Jud. 11:26).
	1211	2	248	
	1210	3	249	
The 1 year of Zama-shum-iddina of Babylon. Invasion by Asshur-daan I of Assyria.	1209	4	250	

NOTES.

a B. C. 1188. Scholars differ as to the place of Nebuchadrezzar among the kings of this dynasty. The place here assigned is the only one that can be given him without making corrections in the Babylonian list of kings. Very likely, however, he was the brains of the preceding reign of 17 years, so that practically his exploits and his rule extended over the whole 23 years.

EXPLANATIONS OF THE DATES.

The chronological numbers are to be found in the references in the column of events.

THE TABLES

Foreign Dated Events.	? B. C.	Jephthah.	A. T. J.	Israelitish Dated Events.
The first of the 3 years of Bel-shum-iddina of Babylon.	1208	5	251	
	1207	6	252	
	1206	1	253	*Ibzan*, of Bethlehem, judge (Jud. 12:8-10).
First year of dynasty of Pashé in Babylon.	1205	2	254	
	1204	3	255	
Mutakkil-nusku in Assyria.	1203	4	256	
	1202	5	257	
	1201	6	258	
	1200	7	259	
	1199	1	260	*Elon*, of Zebulun, judge (Jud. 12: 11-12).
	1198	2	261	
	1197	3	262	
	1196	4	263	
	1195	5	264	
	1194	6	265	
	1193	7	266	
	1192	8	267	
	1191	9	268	
	1190	10	269	
	1189	1	270	*Abdon*, of Ephraim, judge (Jud. 12:13-15).
? Nebuchadnezzar I in Babylon *a* for 6 years (List of kings). He had wars with Asshur-resh-ishi, king of Assyria (*Rec. of Past*, new series, IV, 30).	1188	2	271	
	1187	3	272	
	1186	4	273	
	1185	5	274	
	1184	6	275	

NOTES.

a A. T. J. 278. We may conjecture that the Philistines would not permit a national judge in Israel, and that the functions of judge therefore shifted to the high priest.

b A. T. J. 287. The missing generations in the line of David were before Boaz, not after.

c B. C. 1162. Tiglath-pilezer gives us a very full account of his accession year and the following 5 years (see *Rec. of Past*, new series, I, 86ff). As he does not mention his Babylonian wars, we infer that these six years preceded those wars, by how many years we do not know.

EXPLANATIONS OF THE DATES.

The 40 years of this Philistine oppression seem to have coincided with the 40 years of Eli (Jud. 13:1; 1 Sam. 4:18).

The famine which drove Elimelech's family from Judah, and kept them away 10 years (Ruth 1:4), was of course partly the result of invasions. It belongs to the early part of the oppression, when Israel was struggling against subjugation. After resistance ceased, agricultural prosperity returned.

The marriage of Ruth was not many weeks after their coming to Bethlehem.

At the close of the 40 years Samuel was an influential prophet (1 Sam. 3:19–21). Therefore he must have been born early in the 40 years; but some years after they began (1 Sam. 1:3, 7, etc.).

THE TABLES

Foreign Dated Events.	? B. C.	Abdon.	A. T. J.	Israelitish Dated Events.
	1183	7	276	
	1182	8	277	A third Philistine oppression begins.
	1181	1	278	? Naomi flees to Moab (Ruth). *Eli*, the high priest, acts as judge *a* (1 Sam. 1-4).
	1180	2	279	
	1179	3	280	
	1178	4	281	
	1177	5	282	
	1176	6	283	
	1175	7	284	
Kings of the dynasty of Pashé in Babylon.	1174	8	285	
	1173	9	286	? Naomi returns from Moab. ? Boaz marries Ruth.
	1172	10	287	? Obed born. *b*
	1171	11	288	? Samuel born (1 Sam. 1:1-2:11).
	1170	12	289	
	1169	13	290	
	1168	14	291	The bad conduct of Eli's sons (1 Sam. 2:12-36).
	1167	15	292	
	1166	16	293	
	1165	17	294	
	1164	18	295	
	1163	19	296	
Tiglath-pilezer I on the throne in Assyria. *c*	1162	20	297	
	1161	21	298	
	1160	22	299	? The call of Samuel (1 Sam. 3).
	1159	23	300	

NOTES.

a B. C. 1157. See Introduction 26. Sennacherib says that in B. C. 689 he brought from Babylon the gods which this Marduk had taken thither 418 years before. That this year (1106 B. C. Assyrian, 1157 B. C. in these tables) was the accession year of Marduk, not his first year or later, appears from the fact that he only reigned 1½ years, and that Tiglath-pilezer defeated him in two campaigns.

This date gives us other dates. According to the Babylonian list of kings Marduk's accession year was the 49th year of the dynasty of Pashé, and the preceding, the Kassite, dynasty lasted 577 years nearly. This gives 1782 B. C. (1731 B. C. Assyrian) as the date of the beginning of the Kassite dynasty.

The first 4 kings of this dynasty reigned 68 years, to B. C. 1714. Between 1714 and the accession of Ramman-nadin-ahhi, B. C. 1322 (see note, B. C. 1329), a period of 392 years, the list reckons 19 kings, the reigns averaging nearly 21 years. The last 17 of the 19 names have been lost from the list, but at least 12 of them are known from other sources.

Four of the 19 reigned before Burna-buriash (about 1650 B. C., see note at B. C. 1652): Adu-me-ur, Uzzi-u-mash, Kara-indash, Kallimma-sin. There is not much room for others, though many place here the long reign of Agu-kak-rimi and other actual or conjectural reigns. Burna-buriash can be reconciled with current theories of Egyptian chronology only by the process of putting as many kings before him, and as few after him, as possible.

Among the kings after Burna-buriash were Nazi-bugash the usurper, Kadashman-hharbe, "Kuri-galzu the second," and Nazi-maruttash. How many years they reigned is unknown. Their Assyrian contemporaries were Asshur-uballit, Bel-nirari, Budu-ilu, Ramman-nirari I (see note, B. C. 1628).

Just before Ramman-nadin-ahhi the list places two kings whose names are lost. They reigned 48 years, that is, from B. C. 1370. They, and perhaps their predecessor, were contemporaries of Shalmanezer I of Assyria and his son Tukulti-ninip I.

Between the contemporaries of Ramman-nirari I and those of Shalmanezer I the Babylonian documents place Kadashman-turgu, perhaps Agu-kak-rimi, Kudur-bel and his son Shagashalti-buriash (see note, B. C. 1396), and 3 kings whose names are lost. These are enough to fill all the time required by the chronology of these tables.

EXPLANATIONS OF THE DATES.

The chronological numbers are found in 1 Samuel 4: 18 and 7: 2.

THE TABLES

Foreign Dated Events.	?B.C.	Eli.	A.T.J.	Israelitish Dated Events.
	1158	24	301	
Marduk successful against Assyria. *a*	1157	25	302	
First year of Marduk-nadin-ahhi in Babylon. Defeated by Tiglath-pilezer.	1156	26	303	
Defeated again. Reigned but half the year (*Rec. of Past*, new series I, 17; IV, 30).	1155	27	304	
	1154	28	305	
	1153	29	306	
	1152	30	307	
	1151	31	308	
Kings of the twenty-first dynasty in Egypt.	1150	32	309	
	1149	33	310	
	1148	34	311	
	1147	35	312	
	1146	36	313	
About this time Tiglath-pilezer I was followed by Asshur-bel-kala, whose Babylonian contemporaries were Marduk-shapik-zer-mati and Ramman-aplu-iddina (*Rec. of Past*, new series IV, 31).	1145	37	314	
	1144	38	315	
	1143	39	316	
	1142	40	317	Death of Eli; Israel defeated; the ark captured and returned (1 Sam. 1-6).
	1141	1	318	20 years of waiting (1 Sam. 7:2-4).
	1140	2	319	
	1139	3	320	
	1138	4	321	
	1137	5	322	
	1136	6	323	
	1135	7	324	
	1134	8	325	

NOTES.

a A. T. J. 338. The account of the administration of Samuel is so brief that one might lose sight of the fact that it is represented to have been strong and brilliant. He remained judge all his life (1 Sam. 7: 15), though from the accession of Saul the king was chief magistrate, and the judge was so no longer. "All the days of Samuel" (13) means the days while he was chief magistrate.

The achievements attributed to him in this brief passage are continuous success against the Philistines, the recovery of the Israelitish cities that were in the Philistine country, the terminating of the condition of feud which had till then existed between the Israelites and such of the Amorites as remained in the land, and a systematic arrangement for the administration of justice and of public affairs.

Of the cities in his circuit (1 Sam. 7: 16) Gilgal may have been in the Jordan valley, and Mizpah in Gilead, making the circuit national. And even if one holds that the four cities were all within a few miles of his home, still the account presents his administration as national.

The success of it appears, for example, in the populousness of the country when he turned over the power to Saul (*e. g.* 1 Sam. 11: 8).

EXPLANATIONS OF THE DATES.

For 20 years after the death of Eli, Samuel wisely prefers the part of influential citizen to that of official ruler. Then he sees that the time is ripe for another attempt at independence, so he permits the people to make him chief magistrate. Of course the Philistines interfere by armed force, for a united Israel is a menace to their power over Israel. By Jehovah's help Samuel defeats them signally, and thus establishes his authority.

THE TABLES

Foreign Dated Events.	? B. C.	Interim.	A. T. J.	Israelitish Dated Events.
	1133	9	326	
Close of dynasty of Pashé in Babylon. Followed by the dynasty "of the land of the sea."	1132	10	327	
	1131	11	328	
Perhaps Asshur-bel-kala still king of Assyria.	1130	12	329	
	1129	13	330	
	1128	14	331	
	1127	15	332	
	1126	16	333	
Kings of the twenty-first dynasty in Egypt.	1125	17	334	
	1124	18	335	
	1123	19	336	
	1122	20	337	
	1121	1	338	*Samuel* judge *a* (1 Sam. 7:5-17).
	1120	2	339	
	1119	3	340	
	1118	4	341	
	1117	5	342	
	1116	6	343	
	1115	7	344	
	1114	8	345	
	1113	9	346	
	1112	10	347	
	1111	11	348	
	1110	12	349	
	1109	13	350	

NOTES.

a A. T. J. 357. Samuel remained judge, but the judge was now outranked by the king.

b A. T. J. 358. Had he a military camp for a capital?

c A. T. J. 371. Our information concerning the Philistine "garrison" (1 Sam. 13:3) is too meager to justify inferences.

d A. T. J. 371. The magnitude of the Philistine preparations (1 Sam. 13:5) indicates how formidable Israel had become under the statesmanship of Samuel. But now, owing to the dissensions between Samuel and Saul, Israel seems to have been subjugated by the Philistines without a struggle.

EXPLANATIONS OF THE DATES.

The movement for monarchy covered some years, just before Saul was made king.

The 19 years here assigned to Samuel are simply the interval between the dated events that precede and those that follow. According to the 480 of 1 Kings 6:1, if counted from the beginning of the exodus period, the fourth year of Solomon was the year 440 A. T. J. Counting back through the 4 years of Solomon, the 41 of David (2 Sam. 5:5) and the 40 of Saul (Acts 13:21), we obtain 357 A. T. J. as the first year of Saul (see table).

That Samuel's term can have been neither much longer nor much shorter than these 19 years appears from three facts. He had been many years prominent before the term began; it lasted long enough to give his sons time to prove themselves failures; Samuel lived after it nearly to the end of the reign of Saul.

Make a wide paragraph space between 1 Samuel 13:2 and 13:3. The second verse closes what the narrator has to say concerning the first two years of Saul. Saul is a young man, and Jonathan a little boy, though old enough to be guarded by troops, as the prince royal. This is confirmed by the representation that Abner, Saul's uncle and senior, was not a superannuated man some years after the close of Saul's 40 years.

The date of David's birth is computed by counting his 30th year as the first year of his reign in Hebron (2 Sam. 5:4–5).

The beginning of Saul's wars with the Philistines was after Jonathan became a warrior, soon after, or the events will be too crowded.

Of Saul's exploits as summarized in 1 Samuel 14:47–52, those against Moab, Ammon, the Philistines, Amalek, may be the ones narrated in 1 Samuel. Those against Edom and Zobah are mentioned without date or other details.

THE TABLES

Foreign Dated Events.	? B.C.	Samuel.	A.T.J.	Israelitish Dated Events.
	1108	14	351	
	1107	15	352	
	1106	16	353	
	1105	17	354	
From Asshur-bel-kala to Ramman-nirari II, kings of Assyria, we have the names of a number of Assyrian and Babylonian kings, but the records are too incomplete to follow (see B. C. 963 in these Tables).	1104	18	355	
	1103	19	356	? Movement for monarchy (1 Sam. 8).
	1102	1	357	*Saul* made King *a* (1 Sam. 9-10). His victory over Ammon (1 Sam. 11).
	1101	2	358	Renewal of the kingdom (1 Sam. 11: 14-12: 25).
Kings of the twenty-first dynasty in Egypt.	1100	3	359	Establishing of capital *b* (1 Sam. 13: 1-2).
	1099	4	360	
	1098	5	361	
	1097	6	362	
	1096	7	363	
	1095	8	364	
	1094	9	365	
	1093	10	366	
	1092	11	367	Birth of David.
	1091	12	368	
	1090	13	369	
	1089	14	370	? Philistine wars begin *a* (1 Sam. 13: 3-4).
	1088	15	371	? Great invasion. *d* Israel disarmed (1 Sam. 13: 5-23).
	1087	16	372	
	1086	17	373	
	1085	18	374	? Jonathan's victory (1 Sam. 14).
	1084	19	375	? Saul's wars with Zobah, Edom etc.

Notes.

a A. T. J. 386. Or Pas-dammim. See 1 Samuel 17; 1 Chron. 11: 10–14; 2 Samuel 23: 8–12.

b A. T. J. 386. Saul's attempts on the life of David fall into four series. First, soon after the slaying of Goliath, Saul hurled his spear at David, and afterward transferred him from the court to a post of danger (1 Sam. 18: 6–13).

For probably a year or more following, David's ability and growing popularity made Saul jealous. He made his second series of attempts, extending over some months, stimulating David to reckless deeds that he might fall by the hand of the Philistines (1 Sam. 18: 14–27). The result was that David married into Saul's family.

Saul refrained for a time, and then made a third series of attempts, stirring up his servants to assassinate David (1 Sam. 18: 28–19: 7). He was rebuked by Jonathan, and again received David into favor.

When David again distinguished himself the fourth series began, and the situation became chronic.

c A. T. J. 394. This places Samuel's death 434 years after Israel left Egypt, perhaps the round number 450 of Acts.

Explanations of the Dates.

The war against Amalek and the final break between Samuel and Saul must be placed early enough to allow room for the events of the life of David, who was 30 years old when he became king (2 Sam. 5: 4).

Perhaps David was 16 years old when he was anointed—old enough to tend sheep, but not expected as a man at the sacrificial feast.

Perhaps he was 19 when he first went to Saul with his harp, having already a reputation for wisdom and prowess as well as for minstrelsy.

Perhaps he was 20 when he slew Goliath, and 22 when he married Michal, and 25 when they watched the house to kill him, and Saul's desire for his death became permanent and dominating. See note *b*.

The date of Samuel's death is inferred from the order of the narrative.

David was in the Philistine country "a full year and four months" (1 Sam. 27: 7), going there, apparently, about the beginning of a vernal year, and remaining that year and 4 months of the next. Then came the death of Saul, and after 2 months of negotiations David became king in Hebron (2 Sam. 1: 1–2: 4 and 1 Sam. 30: 26–31). See on page 80ff, *Chronological Problems of David's Reign*.

THE TABLES

Foreign Dated Events.	? B.C.	Saul	A. T. J.	Israelitish Dated Events.
	1083	20	376	
	1082	21	377	
	1081	22	378	
	1080	23	379	
	1079	24	380	
	1078	25	381	? War against Amalek (1 Sam. 15). ? Final break between Samuel and Saul (15:35).
	1077	26	382	? David anointed (1 Sam. 16:1–13).
	1076	27	383	
	1075	28	384	
	1074	29	385	? David goes to Saul with his harp (1 Sam. 16:13–23).
	1073	30	386	? Battle of Ephes-dammim. *a* Goliath. ? Saul's attempts on David, 1st series. *b*
Kings of the twenty-first dynasty in Egypt.	1072	31	387	? Saul's attempts on David, 2d series.
	1071	32	388	? David to marry Merab, but fails. ? David marries Michal.
	1070	33	389	
	1069	34	390	? Saul's attempts on David, 3d series.
	1068	35	391	? Saul's attempts on David, 4th series. ? David an outlaw with 400 men (1 Sam. 22).
	1067	36	392	? David at Keilah with 600 men (1 Sam. 23). ? Saul seeks David in wilderness of Ziph.
	1066	37	393	? The skirt incident (1 Sam. 24).
	1065	38	394	? Death of Samuel, 450 years *c* (Acts 13:19). ? Nabal. The spear and cruse (1 Sam. 25, 26).
	1064	39	395	David 1 year and 4 months in the land of the Philistines (1 Sam. 27–30).
	1063	40	396	Death of Saul (1 Sam. 31; 2 Sam. 1). *David* becomes King in Judah (2 Sam. 2).
	1062	1 2	397	
	1061	3	398	At first negotiations, and then war, between the houses of Saul and David (2 Sam. 2:4*b*–7, and 2:8ff).
	1060	4	399	
	1059	5	400	

Explanations of the Dates.

Ishbosheth's death occurred before the middle of the year, while the wheat harvest was being stored (2 Sam. 4:6). His 2 years (2 Sam. 2:10) were the seventh year of David and part of the eighth. The eighth year, after his death, was occupied with negotiations, and with preparations for crowning David over all Israel at the following new year.

That following year, David's ninth year, was eventful. In it occurred the gathering of the tribes (1 Chron. 12:23–40); the coronation (2 Sam. 5:1–5; 1 Chron. 11:1–3); the taking of Jebus and the promotion of Joab (2 Sam. 5:6–8; 1 Chron. 11:4–6); the return of the people to their homes; the Philistine interference (2 Sam. 5:17–21; 1 Chron. 14:8–12). All these were so early in the year that the Jordan was still in flood.

The Philistines occupied the vicinity of Jerusalem, cutting David off from the northern tribes. Here belongs the water-drawing incident (2 Sam. 23:13b–17; 1 Chron. 11:15b–19). The Gadites somehow got across the swollen Jordan (1 Chron. 12:15), and David, thus reinforced, routed the Philistines.

David's 33 years over all Israel naturally divide themselves into three periods: the period of his wars of defense and conquest, that of rest after the wars, and that of domestic troubles. The third period, beginning with the wrong done to Tamar, is furnished with date numbers (see table and explanations). It occupied the last 12 years of the reign, leaving 21 years for the other two periods.

David's national wars began with the defensive campaign already spoken of against the Philistines. We may be sure that the Philistines did not delay beyond the following year their attempt to retrieve their fortunes (2 Sam. 5:22–25; 1 Chron. 14:13–17). David's four campaigns of conquest (2 Sam. 21:15–17, 18, 19, 20–22, paralleled in 1 Chron. 20) probably followed at once, in successive years, resulting in his suzerainty over Philistia (2 Sam. 8:1; 1 Chron. 18:1).

On these events see further page 80ff, *Chronological Problems of David's Reign*. Not less than 12 years are needed for the Philistine campaigns, the eastern and northern campaigns, and the interval between them; and considerations concerning the age of Solomon forbid the extending of the time more than 2 or 3 years. David's sin in the matter of Uriah seems to belong to the last year of the wars, and his repentance to have been early the following year. The bringing up of the ark and the other events doubtless followed without much delay.

FOREIGN DATED EVENTS.	? B. C.	DAVID.	A. T. J.	ISRAELITISH DATED EVENTS.
	1058	6	401	
	1057	7	402	*Ishbosheth* king 2 years (2 Sam. 2:8–4:12).
	1056	8	403	Ishbosheth slain.
	1055	9	404	*David* king of all Israel (2 Sam. 5; 1 Chron. 11, 12, 14). [For the events see opposite page.]
	1054	10	405	Second defensive war against the Philistines (2 Sam. 5:22-25; 1 Chron. 14:13-17).
	1053	11	406	Four campaigns of conquest in Philistia (2 Sam. 8:1; 1 Chron. 18:1, and details in 2 Sam. 21:15–22; 1 Chron. 20:4-8).
	1052	12	407	
	1051	13	408	
	1050	14	409	
	1049	15	410	
Kings of the twenty-first dynasty in Egypt.	1048	16	411	
	1047	17	412	David's eastern and northern conquests (2 Sam. 8:2-18; 1 Chron. 18:2-17, and details in 2 Sam. 10-12; 1 Chron. 19, etc.). Five or more campaigns.
	1046	18	413	
	1045	19	414	
	1044	20	415	
	1043	21	416	? Uriah (2 Sam. 11). ? Final Ammonite campaign (2 Sam. 12). ? Conquest of Edom.
	1042	22	417	? Bathsheba's child (2 Sam. 12:14-23). ? Bringing up ark (2 Sam. 6; 1 Chron. 13-16.) ? Mephibosheth (2 Sam. 9).
	1041	23	418	? The great promise (2 Sam. 7; 1 Chron. 17). ? Birth of Solomon (2 Sam. 12:24-25).
	1040	24	419	
	1039	25	420	
	1038	26	421	? Vengeance on Saul's sons (2 Sam. 21:1-14).
	1037	27	422	
	1036	28	423	
	1035	29	424	
	1034	30	425	The wrong done to Tamar (2 Sam. 13) and its consequences.

NOTES.

a A. T. J. 434. The message of Gad the prophet concerning the census is the latest recorded incident in his career. The earliest is in the time when Saul is persecuting David (1 Sam. 22: 5; 2 Sam. 24; 1 Chron. 21; cf. 1 Chron. 29: 29; 2 Chron. 29: 25).

b A. T. J. 437. When Solomon says that he is "a little child" he means that he is conscious of being too immature for the responsibilities placed upon him. There is no getting away from the fact that his son Rehoboam was born not later than Solomon's first year.

c A. T. J. 438. The prophet Nathan appears in connection with the affair of Uriah, in the giving of the great promise, in the defeat of the plans of Adonijah, and as a historical and liturgical writer (2 Sam. 12: 7 and 7: 2–17; 1 Chron. 17; Psa. 51; 1 Ki. 1; 1 Chron. 29: 29; 2 Chron. 9: 29, 29: 25).

EXPLANATIONS OF THE DATES.

See page 80ff *Chronological Problems of David's Reign.*

The dating in the table goes on the assumption that the Chronicler is correct in holding that great preparations for the temple were made in David's 40th year (1 Chron. 26: 31), and that in connection with these Solomon was made king (1 Chron. 23: 1), the arrangements culminating in a national gathering (1 Chron. 28: 1–29: 22*a*); and that Absalom's rebellion broke out soon after the close of David's 40th year, shortly before the harvest (2 Sam. 15: 7, 17: 19, 28). In Chronicles the temple arrangements follow the purchase of Ornan's threshing floor, after the pestilence after the census (1 Chron. 21 and 22: 1; cf. 2 Sam. 24). Therefore, the 9 months and 20 days of the census (2 Sam. 24: 8) closed just before wheat harvest (1 Chron. 21: 20; cf. 2 Sam. 24: 22) the 40th year of David, and therefore began before the middle of his 39th year.

Josephus (*Ant.* VII, ix, 1) dates the rebellion of Absalom 4 years after his reconciliation with David. This accords with probability, and it is gratuitous to regard the 4 as a mere variation of the 40 of 2 Sam. 15: 7. This places the reconciliation in the 37th year of David, Absalom's return to Jerusalem 2 years earlier, Amnon's death 3 years yet earlier, and the wrong to Tamar 2 years before that (2 Sam. 14: 28, 13: 38, 23).

For the dates for David's 41st year and for the reign of Solomon see page 120.

THE TABLES

Foreign Dated Events.	? B. C.	David.	A. T. J.	Israelitish Dated Events.
	1033	31	426	
	1032	32	427	Death of Amnon. Absalom 3 years in banishment.
	1031	33	428	
	1030	34	429	
	1029	35	430	Absalom 2 years in seclusion (2 Sam. 14).
	1028	36	431	
	1027	37	432	Absalom conspicuous for 4 years (2 Sam. 15: 1–6 cf. Josephus).
	1026	38	433	
	1025	39	434	The census begun (2 Sam. 24; 1 Chron. 21). The prophet GAD. *a*
	1024	40	435	Three days of pestilence. Preparations for temple (1 Chron. 22–27). Ahithophel and Absalom secretly active.
Kings of the twenty-first dynasty in Egypt.	1023	41	436	[For David's 41st year see page 120.]
	1022	1	437	*Solomon*, first year *b* (1 Ki. 2). ? Pharaoh's daughter (1 Ki. 3:1). Solomon's vision, and his wisdom (1 Ki. 3, 4; 2 Chron. 1).
	1021	2	438	The prophet NATHAN. *c*
	1020	3	439	Death of Shimei (1 Ki. 2: 36–46).
	1019	4	440	Temple founded 2d month, and 7½ years in building (1 Ki. 5–7; 2 Chron. 1–4).
	1018	5	441	
	1017	6	442	
	1016	7	443	
	1015	8	444	
	1014	9	445	
	1013	10	446	
	1012	11	447	Temple finished, 8th month. Solomon's house begun.
	1011	12	448	⎧ Temple dedicated, 7th month (1 Ki. 8; 2 Chron. 5–7). ⎨ ? Solomon's second vision (1 Ki. ⎩ 9: 1–9; 2 Chron. 7: 12–22).
	1010	13	449	
	1009	14	450	

Notes.

a A. T. J. 461ff. The important recorded events of Solomon's great reign are numerous, but the record is mainly in the form of undated general statements. To sort the events and arrange them, on the basis of the nature of each, in their time relations, would require more space than can here be given.

Explanations of the Dates.

The events of the 41st year of David were the following: At the very beginning of the year the assembly when Solomon was recognized as king and the offerings were made for the temple (1 Chron. 28:1–29:22*a*); in the weeks that followed before the harvest on the uplands, the outbreak and spread of the Absalom rebellion (2 Sam. 15–17); later the suppression of the rebellion and the bringing back of David (2 Sam. 18–19); the Sheba affair (2 Sam. 20); the physical and mental breakdown of David (1 Ki. 1); the Adonijah affair, and the making of Solomon king "a second time" (1 Ki. 1; 1 Chron. 29:22*b*–25); David's death (1 Ki. 2); perhaps the birth of Rehoboam (1 Ki. 14:21, cf. 11:42 and note *b* on A. T. J. 437).

Presumably the deaths of Adonijah and Joab, the retirement of Abiathar and Shimei, Solomon's vision, the incident of the two women, and possibly the marriage with Pharaoh's daughter (1 Ki. 2:12–38, 3:2–15, 16–27, 1) all occurred not later than the first year of Solomon. The death of Shimei was 3 years later, counting inclusively (1 Ki. 2:39). For the years following the numbers explicitly affirm that the temple was founded the fourth year of Solomon, that it was 7 years in building, that it was finished in the 8th month of his 11th year, that it was dedicated in the 7th month of a year, presumably his 12th, that he was 13 years in building his own house, and 20 years in building the two (1 Ki. 6:1, 37, 38, 7:1, 8:2, 9:10).

THE TABLES

FOREIGN DATED EVENTS.	? B. C.	SOLOMON.	A. T. J.	ISRAELITISH DATED EVENTS.
	1008	15	451	
	1007	16	452	
	1006	17	453	
	1005	18	454	
	1004	19	455	
	1003	20	456	
	1002	21	457	
	1001	22	458	
	1000	23	459	Solomon's palace completed (1 Ki. 9:10; 2 Chron. 8:1).
	999	24	460	
At about this time Sheshonk I (Shishak) establishes the 22d dynasty in Egypt.	998	25	461	As the years pass, Solomon's splendid and enterprising reign degenerates, becoming luxurious, idolatrous, oppressive (1 Ki. 9–11; 2 Chron. 8–10). *a*
	997	26	462	
	996	27	463	
	995	28	464	? Queen of Sheba (1 Ki. 10; 2 Chron. 9).
	994	29	465	
	993	30	466	
	992	31	467	
	991	32	468	
? Hadad in Edom and Rezon in Damascus become influential against Solomon (1 Ki. 11:14–25).	990	33	469	
	989	34	470	
	988	35	471	
	987	36	472	
	986	37	473	Disintegrating processes (1 Ki. 11). ? Jeroboam flees to Shishak (1 Ki. 11:26-40).
	985	38	474	
	984	39	475	

Notes.

a B. C. 983. Sheshonk I, the Shishak of the Bible, was the founder of a new dynasty in Egypt. The policy of the preceding dynasty seems to have been one of friendliness to both Solomon and his opponents (1 Ki. 3: 1, 11: 14–22). The Bible says that Shishak received Jeroboam when he fled from Solomon, and that he invaded Judah (1 Ki. 11: 40, 14: 25, and details in 2 Chron. 12: 2–10); but it does not necessarily follow that he was friendly to the northern kingdom. On the great Karnak relief he claims to have conquered many cities of both kingdoms.

Near the close of his 21st year he commissioned his priestly chief of public works to build for him the Karnak monument, now so celebrated. The work, from the quarry to the completed decoration, must have required several years, and he claims to have completed it (Breasted, *Ancient Records*, IV, 706, 721). Probably his reign was nearer 30 years in length than 20.

He gives no date for his operations in Palestine. The general guess is that his invasion of Judah in Rehoboam's fifth year was not many years before Shishak's twenty-first year.

See Introduction Chapter IV, especially 24.

Explanations of the Dates.

The duration of the reign of Solomon was 40 years (1 Ki. 11: 42). For the dates of Jeroboam and Rehoboam see the first pages of the next table.

Foreign Dated Events.	? B.C.	Jeroboam.	Solomon.	A. T. J.	Israelitish Dated Events.
Sheshonk I, king of Egypt. a	983		40	476	Death of Solomon and accession of Rehoboam. Secession of Jeroboam and 10 tribes. First year of Jeroboam and of Rehoboam.
	982	1	1	477	
	981	2	2	478	
	980	3	3	479	Rehoboam forsakes the way of David.
	979	4	4	480	
	978	5	5	481	Invasion by Shishak.
	977	6	6	482	
	976	7	7	483	
	975	8	8	484	
	974	9	9	485	
	973	10	10	486	

THIRD TABLE

THE DISRUPTION TO THE CLOSE OF OLD TESTAMENT HISTORY

Notes.

a Head of column A. Di. stands for *Anno Discidii*, the year of the disruption of Israel into the two kingdoms of Israel and Judah.

b Head of column. The synchronisms of the Israelitish and Assyrian dated events now become exact (see at B. C. 910). To reduce the biblical years B. C. to the Assyrian as now commonly received, subtract 51 (see Introduction 23, 27, 34).

c A. Di. 4. Ahijah gave a message to Jeroboam before the death of Solomon, and another later; he was a writer; and possibly the father of king Baasha (1 Ki. 11:29–39, 12:15, 14:2–18, 15:29, 33; 2 Chron. 10:15, 9:29).

Jedo (not Iddo) appears as a writer in 2 Chronicles 9:29. He is probably the prophet from Judah of 1 Kings 13, whom Josephus calls Jadon.

Shemaiah forbade Rehoboam's making war against Israel, rebuked him in the time of Shishak, and wrote his history (1 Ki. 12:22; 2 Chron. 11:2, 12:5–7, 15).

d A. Di. 5. Concerning Shishak see Introduction 24, 27, and note at B. C. 983.

e B. C. 963. At this point the Assyrian eponym canon (see Introduction 10, 23) becomes continuous. I follow George Smith in making 911 B. C. Assyrian (962 B. C. biblical) the eponym year of Rammannirari II, and the preceding year therefore his first year.

See B. C. 1104 in these tables.

f A. Di. 21. The Septuagint is mistaken in dating Asa the 24th year of Jeroboam.

Explanations of the Dates.

Solomon's reign extended to 40 years (1 Ki. 11:42). Doubtless the division into two kingdoms occurred at once, though the details may have extended over several years. The introduction of the calf worship may have been gradual, but we must think that Jeroboam began this policy at once.

Rehoboam was faithful 3 years (2 Chron. 11:17, 12:1). In his 5th year was the Shishak invasion (1 Ki. 14:25; 2 Chron. 12:2).

Rehoboam reigned 17 years (1 Ki. 14:21). The first of Abijam's 3 years was the 18th year of Jeroboam (1 Ki. 15:1, 2). Asa's accession year (1 Ki. 15:9) was the 20th year of Jeroboam, his first year beginning the following new year, as the subsequent numbers prove (see Introduction, Chapter III).

Jeroboam reigned 22 years (1 Ki. 14:20). Nadab succeeded him the second year of Asa (1 Ki. 15:25). That year is counted as the 22d year of Jeroboam, but it is also counted as the first year of Nadab. In actual time Nadab's 2 years are the closing part of the 2d year of Asa, and the opening part of Asa's 3d year. Asa's 3d year is also counted as the first year of Baasha (1 Ki. 15:33).

Foreign Dated Events.	? B.C. b	Assyria.	Israel. Jeroboam I.	Judah. Rehoboam.	A. Di. a	Israelitish Dated Events.
931 B. C. Assyrian.	982		1	1	1	The disruption (1 Ki. 11, 12; 2 Chron. 10, 11). *Jeroboam* (1 Ki. 12-14). *Rehoboam* (1 Ki. 14:21-31; 2 Chron. 11-12). Bethel and Dan established.
	981		2	2	2	
	980		3	3	3	Rehoboam forsakes Jehovah.
	979		4	4	4	The prophets AHIJAH, JEDO, SHEMAIAH. *c*
	978		5	5	5	Invasion by Shishak. *d*
About this time Sheshonk I, late in his 21st year, commissions Haremsaf to build the Karnak structure.	977		6	6	6	
	976		7	7	7	
	975		8	8	8	
	974		9	9	9	
	973		10	10	10	
	972		11	11	11	
	971		12	12	12	
About this time began the 36 or more years of Osorkon I of Egypt.	970		13	13	13	
	969		14	14	14	
	968	RAMMAN NIRARI II.	15	15	15	
	967		16	16	16	
	966		17	17	17	Death of Rehoboam. Accession of Abijam.
	965		18	1	18	*Abijam* (1 Ki. 15:1-8; 2 Chron. 13).
Death of Asshur-daan II of Assyria. Accession of Ramman-nirari II. *e*	964		19	2	19	
	963	1	20	3	20	Death of Abijam. Accession of Asa.
He was in relations with Shamash-mudammiq and his successor Nabu-shumishkun, kings of Babylon (*Rec. of Past*, new series, IV, 32).	962	2	21	1	21	*Asa* (1 Ki. 15:9-24; 2 Chron. 14-16). *f*
	961	3	22/1	2	22	Death of Jeroboam. Accession of Nadab. *Nadab* (1 Ki. 15:25-32).
	960	4	2/1	3	23	Death of Nadab. Accession of Baasha. *Baasha* (1 Ki. 15:16-16:7).
	959	5	2	4	24	
	958	6	3	5	25	

NOTES.

a A. Di. 36. "And war not having occurred to the 35th year of the kingdom of Asa, in the 36th year of the kingdom of Asa, Baasha, king of Israel, came up upon Judah" (2 Chron. 15: 19, 16: 1). Not "no more war," as in the English versions. The writer is speaking of war with Israel, not with other countries. During the 15 years of which he has been speaking there has been no war with Israel, but war began the following year. Either the numbers 35 and 36 are to be corrected, or they give the date in terms starting from the disruption.

Josephus perhaps made the dates the 25th and 26th of Asa. He says: "So after this Baasha had no leisure to make expeditions against Asa, for he was prevented by death" (*Ant.* VIII, xii, 4). But this is not so well.

b A. Di. 37ff. Oded and his son Azariah prophesied to Asa (2 Chron. 15: 1–8).

Hanani rebuked Asa for seeking assistance from Benhadad (2 Chron. 16: 7).

Jehu, the son of Hanani, testified against Baasha, inspired Jehoshaphat to his work of reform, wrote history that was inserted in the book of the Kings (1 Ki. 16: 1, 7, 12; 2 Chron. 19: 2, 20: 34).

EXPLANATIONS OF THE DATES.

Jehoshaphat was 35 years old the first year of his reign (1 Ki. 22: 42), A. Di. 62.

Asa's reign began with 10 years of quiet (2 Chron. 14: 1).

The cattle captured in the Zerah war were used in the sacrifices the 3d month of the 15th year of Asa (2 Chron. 15: 10). Therefore, the invasion either began the preceding year, or extended over more years than one.

For the date of the Baasha war see note *a*.

Baasha reigned 24 years (1 Ki. 15: 33). His 24th year was the 26th of Asa, and was also the first of the 2 years of Elah (1 Ki. 16:8). Elah's 2d year was the 27th of Asa, in the course of which he was slain by Zimri (1 Ki. 16: 10, 15). The same year was the first of the 12 years of Omri, which terminated in the 38th of Asa (1 Ki. 16: 23, 29). The 31st year of Asa is also given as the date of Omri's accession. It is possible to infer that Omri became sole king at that date, Tibni's rivalry having lasted the 4 intervening years.

That the Tyrian alliance and the marriage of Ahab and Jezebel occurred very early in Omri's reign is inferred from the fact that a grandson of that marriage was 22 years old in A. Di. 90, which see.

THE TABLES

Foreign Dated Events.	? B. C.	Assyria. Ramman-nirari.	Israel. Baasha.	Judah. Asa.	A. Di.	Israelitish Dated Events.
906 B. C. Assyrian.	957	7	4	6	26	
	956	8	5	7	27	Jehoshaphat born.
	955	9	6	8	28	
	954	10	7	9	29	
	953	11	8	10	30	Close of 10 years of quiet.
	952	12	9	11	31	
	951	13	10	12	32	
	950	14	11	13	33	
	949	15	12	14	34	? Invasion by Zerah (2 Chron. 14:9ff).
Zerah the Cushite must have been either Osorkon I or his ally.	948	16	13	15	35	Final defeat of Zerah. Great festival. 3d month. Up to this time no war with Israel.
	947	17	14	16	36	War with Baasha and Israel *a* (1 Ki. 15:16-22; 2 Chron. 15:19-16:10).
	946	18	15	17	37	The prophets, ODED, AZARIAH, HANANI, JEHU. *b*
	945	19	16	18	38	
	944	20	17	19	39	
	943	21	18	20	40	
Death of Ramman-nirari II. Accession of Tukulti-ninip II.	942	22	19	21	41	
	941	1	20	22	42	
	940	2	21	23	43	
	939	3	22	24	44	
	938	4	23	25	45	
	937	5	24/1	26	46	Baasha dies. Accession of Elah. *Elah* and *Zimri* (1 Ki. 16:8-20).
Death of Tukulti-ninip II. Accession of Asshur-nazir-pal.	936	6	2/1	27	47	Elah dies. Accession of Zimri. Zimri dies. Accession of Omri.
His reign of 25 years was from the outset a series of conquests.	935	1	2	28	48	Tibni contests the crown. *Omri* and *Tibni* (1 Ki. 16:21-28).
See his standard inscription in *Rec. of Past*, new series, II.	934	2	3	29	49	? Tyrian alliance formed. ? Ahab marries Jezebel.
About this time began the 23 or more years of Takelot I, of Egypt.	933	3	4	30	50	

NOTES.

a A. Di. 61. Some Greek copies date Jehoshaphat the 11th year of Omri, and Ahab the 2d year of Jehoshaphat. Very likely these numbers are correct as indicating a coreign. If so, it is not included in the 25 years attributed to Jehoshaphat.

b A. Di. 65. We have no information as to the beginnings of the careers of these two celebrated prophets. Their contest with Jezebel for influence over Ahab began early.

c B. C. 910. The synchronism is at this point perfectly definite. Shalmanezer says that in his 6th year he defeated the allies Benhadad and Ahab, and in his 18th year he received tribute from Jehu. Hence his 18th year cannot have been earlier than the accession year of Jehu, and his 6th year cannot have been later than the 21st of Ahab, for Ahab and Benhadad were never allies after that. The synchronism can be moved neither backward nor forward by so much as one year.

EXPLANATIONS OF THE DATES.

The Moabite stone says that Omri and his sons oppressed Moab 40 years. Hence the oppression began not later than the 40th year before the close of the dynasty.

Jehoram was born 32 years before he became king (2 Ki. 8: 17).

Omri founded Samaria after reigning 6 years (1 Ki. 16: 23).

Omri 12 years (1 Ki. 16: 23). Ahab's accession year and first year was the 38th of Asa (1 Ki. 16: 29). Asa's disease was in his 39th year (2 Chron. 16: 12), and his reign was 41 years (1 Ki. 15: 10). Jehoshaphat became king the 4th year of Ahab (1 Ki. 22: 41), but the subsequent numbers prove that his first year is counted from the following new year. His teaching mission was in his 3d year (2 Chron. 17: 7–9).

The sudden appearance of Elijah (1 Ki. 17) implies previous relations with Ahab, presumably for years. Elisha was an old acquaintance of the Shunammite family when their child was born.

Jehoram and Athaliah were married early enough so that their son Ahaziah was 22 years old in A. Di. 90, which see.

The restoration of the Shunammite boy occurred more than 7 years before the death of Benhadad and of Joram, king of Israel, (2 Ki. 8: 1–8); hence his birth was some years before the close of the reign of Ahab. It was before the relations of Ahab with the prophets ceased to be friendly.

The $3\frac{1}{2}$ years (1 Ki. 18: 1; Luke 4: 25; Ja. 5: 17) of Elijah's seclusion must have been an appreciable time before the close relations of the prophets to the king in the Syrian wars (1 Ki. 20).

THE TABLES

Foreign Dated Events.	? B. C.	Assyria. Asshur-nazir-pal.	Israel. Omri.	Judah. Asa.	A. Di.	Israelitish Dated Events.
881 B. C. Assyrian.	932	4	5	31	51	Omri sole king on death of Tibni. He conquers Moab. Jehoram, of Judah, born. Samaria founded.
	931	5	6	32	52	
Asshur-nazir-pal in conflict with Nabu-aplu-iddina of Babylon.	930	6	7	33	53	
	929	7	8	34	54	
	928	8	9	35	55	
At various dates Asshurnazir-pal represents himself as invading the countries on the eastern coast of the Mediterranean, taking tribute from the Phoenicians, among others, and carrying off timber from Lebanon.	927	9	10	36	56	
	926	10	11	37	57	
	925	11	12 1	38	58	Death of Omri. Accession of Ahab. *Ahab* (1 Ki. 16:29-22:51).
	924	12	2	39	59	Asa diseased in his feet.
	923	13	3	40	60	
	922	14	4	41	61	Death of Asa. Accession of Jehoshaphat. *a* Baalism now prevalent in Israel.
	921	15	5	1	62	*Jehoshaphat* (1 Ki. 22; 2 Ki. 1-3; 2 Chron. 17-20).
	920	16	6	2	63	
	919	17	7	3	64	Jehoshaphat's teaching mission (2 Chron. 17).
	918	18	8	4	65	? The prophets Elijah and Elisha. *b* (1 Ki. 17 to 2 Ki. 13).
	917	19	9	5	66	
	916	20	10	6	67	Marriage of Jehoram and Athaliah.
	915	21	11	7	68	Ahaziah of Judah born.
	914	22	12	8	69	
	913	23	13	9	70	? Shunammite's son promised (2 Ki. 4).
Death of Asshur-nazirpal. Accession of Shalmanezer II.	912	24	14	10	71	? Shunammite's son born. ? Elijah goes to Cherith. (1 Ki. 17: 1-7).
	911	25	15	11	72	? Elijah goes to Zarephath (1 Ki. 17: 8-24).
There have been preserved to us the records, *c* year by year, of his exploits, for a large part of his long reign. See *Rec. of Past*, new series, II and IV.	910	1	16	12	73	
	909	2	17	13	74	? The slaughter at Carmel. Elijah's flight. The call of Elisha (1 Ki. 18-19).
	908	3	18	14	75	

NOTES.

a A. Di. 79, Explanations. Concerning Micaiah, otherwise Micah, and Eliezer and Jahaziel, we have only the information given in the passages here cited.

b A. Di. 86. Presumably Naaman was the brains of the Benhadad confederacy, which resisted Shalmanezer for so many years.

c A. Di. 96. Some Greek copies date Joash in the 8th year of Jehu, possibly counting Jehu's accession year as his first year.

EXPLANATIONS OF THE DATES.

For Osorkon see the preceding Egyptian dates. For Shalmanezer see his inscriptions (e. g., *Rec. of Past*, old series III, new series IV), and the accounts of him under "Assyria" in the large Bible Dictionaries.

The second victory of Ahab was at "the turn of the year," that is, the autumnal equinox. The Naboth affair is here dated from the order of the narrative. The "third year" of the 3 years of peace (1 Ki. 22: 1–2) was the last year of Ahab, making the 3 years to be A. Di. 77, 78, 79. The fighting of 1 Ki. 20 occurred not long before the 3 years. Syria and Israel fought one another in the odd years when they were not in alliance to fight the Assyrian.

Ahaziah's 2 years were the 17th and 18th of Jehoshaphat (1 Ki. 22: 51; 2 Ki. 3: 1). As these years are included in the 22 years of Ahab (1 Ki. 16: 29), it is a case of coregnancy. Perhaps Ahab associated his son with himself as a precaution before the war against Shalmanezer.

The hypothesis that Jehoshaphat made a like arrangement with his son Jehoram, and repudiated it afterward, would explain the otherwise misfitting statement (2 Ki. 1: 17) that Joram of Israel became king the 2d year of Jehoram of Judah.

The 18th year of Jehoshaphat is both the accession year and the first year of Joram of Israel (2 Ki. 3: 1), so that this year is counted three times—to Ahab, to Ahaziah, to Joram.

The events of the year 79 A. Di. seem to have had their beginnings in the following order. Of course they overlapped.

Jehoshaphat in alliance with Ahab (1 Ki. 22: 2–40; 2 Chron. 18). MICAIAH, son of Imlah.*a*

His visit "at an end of years" (2 Chron. 18: 2).

Ramoth-gilead. Death of Ahab.

Jehoshaphat's partnership in commerce with Ahaziah (1 Ki. 22: 48–49; 2 Chron. 20: 35–37). ELIEZER, son of Dodavah.*a* Jehoshaphat's judging reformation (2 Chron. 19). His son Jehoram turned down(?).

Revolt of Moab (2 Ki. 1: 1, 3: 5).

Death of Ahaziah of Israel. Fire from heaven (2 Ki. 1).

Invasion by Moab and allies (2 Chron. 20). JAHAZIEL.*a*

Edom changes from deputy to king (1 Ki. 22: 47; cf. 2 Ki. 3).

In the following year, probably, the expedition against Mesha (1 Ki. 3).

(Continued on page 134.)

THE TABLES

Foreign Dated Events.	? B.C.	Assyria. Shalm. II.	Israel. Ahab.	Judah. Jehoshaphat.	A. Di.	Israelitish Dated Events.
856 B. C. Assyrian. About this time began the 30 or more years of Osorkon II, of Egypt.	907	4	19	15	76	Ahab defeats Benhadad twice (1 Ki. 20).
	906	5	20	16	77	Naboth (1 Ki. 21). Three years of peace between Israel and Syria.
Shalmanezer defeats the Benhadad-Ahab alliance.	905	6	1|21	17	78	*Ahaziah* 2 years coregnant with Ahab. Jehoram coregnant with Jehoshaphat(?).
	904	7	2|22 1	18	79	Death of Ahab. Ahaziah sole king. Death of Ahaziah. Accession of Joram. *Joram* of Israel (1 Ki. 1-9).
Shalmanezer defeats Marduk-bel-usati, of Babylon.	903	8	2	19	80	[For events of A. Di. 79, 80, see opposite page.]
Shalmanezer slays Marduk.	902	9	3	20	81	
Shalmanezer defeats Benhadad and allies.	901	10	4	21	82	*Jehoram* coregnant with Jehoshaphat.
He again defeats Benhadad and allies.	900	11	5	1|22	83	*Jehoram* of Judah (2 Ki. 8:16-24; 2 Chron. 21).
	899	12	6	2|23	84	Translation of Elijah (2 Ki. 2). Miracles of Elisha (2 Ki. 2-7).
	898	13	7	3|24	85	Fighting between Syria and Israel (2 Ki. 5:2).
He again defeats these allies.	897	14	8	4|25	86	? Naaman *b* (2 Ki. 5).
	896	15	9	5	87	
	895	16	10	6	88	Fighting between Syria and Israel (2 Ki. 6-7).
	894	17	11	7	89	Jehoram sick 2 years.
Shalmanezer defeats Hazael, and receives tribute from Jehu and others.	893	18	12	8	90	Death of Jehoram. Accession of Ahaziah. *Ahaziah* in Judah (2 Ki. 8:25-29; 2 Chron. 22).
	892	19	1	1	91	Death of Joram. Accession of Jehu. Death of Ahaziah. Accession of Athaliah.
	891	20	2	2	92	*Jehu* in Israel (2 Ki. 9-10).
Shalmanezer defeats Hazael. Tribute from Phoenicia.	890	21	3	3	93	*Athaliah* in Judah (2 Ki. 11; 2 Chron. 22:10ff).
	889	22	4	4	94	
	888	23	5	5	95	
	887	24	6	6	96	Death of Athaliah. Accession of Joash. *c*
	886	25	7	1	97	*Joash* in Judah (2 Ki. 11-12; 2 Chron. 23-24). JEHOIADA.
	885	26	8	2	98	
After the downfall of the dynasty of Omri came the successes of Mesha against Israel, as recorded on the Moabite stone, covering some years.	884	27	9	3	99	In Jehu's reign and later, Israel suffered from Hazael, the Moabites, etc. (2 Ki. 10:32-33, 13:20; Amos 1:3-2:4; cf. 2 Ki. 8:12).
	883	28	10	4	100	

NOTES.

a B. C. 876. For the Assyrian dates see copies of the Eponym Canon (*e. g.*, George Smith's *Assyrian Canon*). For Shamash-ramman and Ramman-nirari, see inscription of the former in *Rec. of Past*, old series I, 9, and Synchronous History in *Rec. of Past*, new series IV, 33–35, 26.

b A. Di. 119. Josephus (*Ant.* IX, viii, 5) makes the reign of Jehoahaz to begin the 21st of Joash, and gives other numbers to match this. His numerals, if accepted, would shorten the chronology by 2 years, and there would be no misfit till we reach the later long numbers.

EXPLANATIONS OF THE DATES.

(*Continued from page 132.*)

The first year of Jehoram of Judah was the 5th of Joram of Israel, and his 8 years closed at the end of a year (2 Chron. 21: 19), at the change from the 11th year of Joram to the 12th (2 Ki. 8: 16, 17, 25 and 9: 29).

In actual time Ahaziah's reign occupied only a small fraction of the year that is counted to him, the year 90 A. Di.; and the last year of Joram's reign consisted of only a similar fraction of the same year. Early in that year Jehu and Athaliah waded in blood to their respective thrones, the first year of each being counted from the following new year.

Note that the biblical and the Assyrian accounts synchronize exactly in the simultaneous disappearance of Benhadad and the dynasty of Omri, and their replacement by Hazael and Jehu.

Athaliah reigned 6 years, and the first year of Joash was the 7th of Jehu (2 Ki 11: 3–4, 12: 1; 2 Chron. 22: 12, 23: 1).

On the Moabite stone (see *e. g.*, *Rec. of Past*, new series II, or the large Bible Dictionaries), the successes of Mesha are dated after the dynasty of Omri had oppressed Moab 40 years. Hence they all belong to a later time than the events of 2 Kings 3.

The close of the reign of Shalmanezer II was disturbed by revolts, and the history is obscure.

Amaziah was 25 years old when his reign began, A. Di. 137 (2 Ki. 14: 2; 2 Chron. 25: 1). The marriages of Joash were early enough for this; in view of his age they cannot have been much earlier.

Jehu reigned 28 years (2 Ki. 10: 36). The first year of Jehoahaz was the 23d of Joash (2 Ki. 13: 1). The renewed interest in the temple is dated from the 23d year of Joash (2 Ki. 12: 6).

THE TABLES

Foreign Dated Events.	? B. C.	Assyria. Shalm. II.	Israel. Jehu.	Judah. Joash.	A. Di.	Israelitish Dated Events.
831 B. C. Assyrian. About this time began in Egypt the 7 years in which Takelot II reigned with Osorkon II.	882	29	11	5	101	
	881	30	12	6	102	
	880	31	13	7	103	
	879	32	14	8	104	
	878	33	15	9	105	
	877	34	16	10	106	
Death of Shalmanezer II? Accession of Shamash-ramman. *a*	876	35	17	11	107	
About this time began the 18 or more years of the sole reign of Takelot II.	875	1	18	12	108	
Shamash-ramman subdued revolts in his 1st year, marched to the Mediterranean his 2d and 3d years, and in his 4th year defeated Marduk-baladhsu-ikbi of Babylon.	874	2	19	13	109	
	873	3	20	14	110	
	872	4	21	15	111	
	871	5	22	16	112	? Jehoiada takes wives for Joash.
	870	6	23	17	113	Amaziah born.
	869	7	24	18	114	
	868	8	25	19	115	
	867	9	26	20	116	
	866	10	27	21	117	Before Jehu's death Hazael has control of the country east of the Jordan (2 Ki. 10:33).
	865	11	28	22	118	Death of Jehu. Accession of Jehoahaz.
	864	12	1	23	119	Jehoahaz in Israel (2 Ki. 13:1-9).*b* Temple repairs in Judah.
Bau-ahh-iddina of Babylon conquered by the Assyrians. Death of Shamash-ramman. Accession of Ramman-nirari III.	863	13	2	24	120	
	862	1	3	25	121	
	861	2	4	26	122	
	860	3	5	27	123	
	859	4	6	28	124	
	858	5	7	29	125	

NOTES.

a A. Di. 133. Jehoash and Joash, like Jehoram and Joram, are mere variant spellings of the same name; but it is convenient to use one spelling for the Israelitish name, and the other for the Judahite.

b A. Di. 135. The historical situation in the book of Joel accurately fits the time of the invasion by Hazael, and that is the strongest known indication of the date of the prophet.

c A. Di. 149. The book of Obadiah presents two historical situations, one the same with that of Joel, the other that of a signal punishment inflicted on Edom.

d B. C. 833. See Introduction 23. Thus far we have followed the exact synchronism established for the time of Shalmanezer II and Ahab and Jehu. The next accurately ascertained synchronism is that between Sargon and the downfall of Samaria. Backward from that the Assyrian dates are continuous to the first year of Asshur-daan III, B. C. 772. For the interval between Ramman-nirari and Asshur-daan the Assyrian Canon has only the 10 years of Shalmanezer III, while the biblical numbers make the time to be 61 years, and specify, though briefly, the events that occupied those years.

If we place Shalmanezer immediately before Asshur-daan, the preceding 51 years, from the point of view of the Assyrian Canon, have no existence, and the events which the Bible assigns to them have to be distributed through the decades that follow, in some instances crowding out of place the events which the Bible assigns to those decades.

For these reasons we drop the Assyrian column from the table for the next two pages, and for those and the following pages add a column giving the years B. C. to which Assyriologists assign the biblical events. Most of the dates in that column are taken from the article on "Chronology" in the Hastings Bible Dictionary.

EXPLANATIONS OF THE DATES.

The incident of Zechariah must have occurred late in the reign of Joash.

Jehoash of Israel the 37th year of Joash of Judah (2 Ki. 13: 10). That this was the beginning of a coreign of 3 years, not counted in the 16 years of Jehoash, appears from the statement that Amaziah lived 15 years after the death of Jehoash (2 Ki. 14: 17; 2 Chron. 25: 25).

Jehoahaz 17 years (2 Ki. 13: 1), Joash of Judah 40 years (2 Ki. 12: 1), Amaziah 2d year of Jehoash of Israel (2 Ki. 14: 1).

The *Seder Olam* (19) says that Amaziah's invasion of Edom was made in his 12th year, and this is as likely a date as any. His defeat by Jehoash occurred at some time between the Edom affair and his death (2 Ki. 14; 2 Chron. 25).

THE TABLES

Foreign Dated Events.	B. C.	Assyria. Ramman-N.	Israel. Jehoahaz.	Judah. Joash.	A. Di.	Israelitish Dated Events.
B. C. 806 Assyrian. About this time begin the 52 years of Sheshonk III in Egypt.	857	6	8	30	126	
	856	7	9	31	127	
	855	8	10	32	128	
	854	9	11	33	129	
	853	10	12	34	130	
	852	11	13	35	131	
	851	12	14	36	132	Zechariah, son of Jehoiada (2 Chron. 24: 20).
	850	13	15	37	133	Jehoash *a*, of Israel, coregnant with Jehoahaz.
	849	14	16	38	134	
Expedition of Rammannirari to Manzuat (Eponym Canon). Scholars conjecture that this was the expedition in which he says that he took tribute from the entire region west of the Euphrates, "Tyre, Sidon, the land Omri, Edom, Philistia, As far as the great sea to the setting of the sun;" and that he humbled Mariha the king of Damascus (see *e. g.* Smith's *Canon*, p. 115). Mariha means "lord," and Mariha may have been Hazael, or Benhadad who succeeded him about the beginning of the reign of Jehoash (2 Ki. 13: 22-25).	848	15	17	39	135	{ Hazael's expedition. ? Joel. *b* Death of Jehoahaz. Accession of Jehoash. ? Death of Elisha.
	847	16	1	40	136	{ *Jehoash* in Israel (2 Ki. 13-14). Death of Joash. Accession of Amaziah.
	846	17	2	1	137	*Amaziah* in Judah (2 Ki. 14; 2 Chron. 25).
	845	18	3	2	138	? Victories of Jehoash over Damascus (2 Ki. 13: 24-25).
	844	19	4	3	139	
	843	20	5	4	140	[Ussher makes the 41 years of Jeroboam II begin the 4th year of Amaziah, the first 11 years being a coreign. Thus he closes the gap between Amaziah and Uzziah. His date for the 4th of Amaziah is 836 B. C.]
	842	21	6	5	141	
	841	22	7	6	142	
	840	23	8	7	143	
	839	24	9	8	144	
	838	25	10	9	145	
	837	26	11	10	146	
	836	27	12	11	147	
	835	28	13	12	148	? Amaziah beats Edom.
Here begins the divergence between the biblical and Assyrian chronology. *d*	834	29	14	13	149	? Obadiah. *c*
	833		15	14	150	? Jehoash beats Amaziah.

Notes.

a A. Di 153. The writer of the book of Jonah has presented accurately the values of the historical situation. It was the unknown disasters in Assyria, just after Ramman-nirari had broken the power of Damascus, that rendered the successes of Jeroboam possible.

b B. C. 825. At the beginning of this blank period the Assyrians, under Ramman-nirari, are taking tribute from the whole Mediterranean region, Judah excepted. At its close we find a situation in which their power over the region has been lost, and they are engaged in a desperate struggle to regain it.

Explanations of the Dates.

The reign of Jehoash of Israel lasted 16 years (2 Ki. 13: 10). Jeroboam's first year was the 15th of Amaziah (2 Ki. 14: 23). Ussher counts this as the date of Jeroboam's sole reign, and holds that his 41 years began 11 years earlier.

The writer in Kings places Jonah early enough so that he promised the successes which Jeroboam achieved. Probably these began early in his reign. The preaching of Jonah may have been a large factor in them.

Uzziah was 16 years old when he became king, A. Di. 177 (2 Ki. 15: 1-2).

Amaziah reigned 29 years (2 Ki. 14: 2). Perhaps his reign was merely nominal from the time when Jehoash defeated him and broke down the walls of Jerusalem. Jehoash and Jeroboam seem to have used their successes wisely, and thus to have maintained a dominant influence in Judah.

THE TABLES

Foreign Dated Events.	? B. C.	Israel. Jehoash.	? B. C. Assyrian.	Judah. Amaziah.	A. D.	Israelitish Dated Events.
Between this date and B. C. 720 the second half of the 52 years of Sheshonk III, the 6 years and more of Pemou, the 37 years and more of Sheshonk IV, the 23 years and more of Pedibast, the 14 years and more of Osorkon III, the 6 years and more of Bekneranef, perhaps other kings, and the beginning of the reign of Shabaka.	832	16 1	782	15	151	Death of Jehoash. Accession of Jeroboam. *Jeroboam II* in Israel (2 Ki. 14).
	831	2		16	152	
	830	3		17	153	?JONAH (2 Ki. 14:25). *a*
	829	4		18	154	
	828	5		19	155	
	827	6		20	156	
	826	7		21	157	
Here the Assyrian records are virtually a blank. The period, whether a few years only or several decades, was a period of disaster (see note at B. C. 765). *b*	825	8		22	158	
	824	9		23	159	
	823	10		24	160	In these years Jeroboam II becomes suzerain of all the peoples from the Mediterranean to the Euphrates.
	822	11		25	161	
	821	12		26	162	Birth of Uzziah.
	820	13		27	163	
	819	14		28	164	
	818	15	767	29	165	Death of Amaziah. Interregnum in Judah 11 years.
	817	16			166	
	816	17			167	
	815	18			168	
	814	19			169	
	813	20			170	
	812	21			171	
	811	22			172	
	810	23			173	
	809	24			174	
	808	25			175	

Notes.

a B. C. Assyrian 741. Dr. J. Taylor in "Amos" in the *Dictionary of the Bible* dates the death of Jeroboam about 750 B. C., and the prophesying of Amos about 760 B. C.

Dr. A. B. Davidson in "Hosea" in the same *Dictionary* dates the death of Jeroboam about B. C. 746–745, and the beginning of Hosea's ministry "some time previous."

b A. Di. 191. Here the Bible numbers indicate an interregnum of 22 years in Israel —quite in accord with Hosea's program.

Explanations of the Dates.

Uzziah's reign began the 27th year of Jeroboam II (2 Ki. 15: 1). Ussher dates this not from the beginning of Jeroboam's reign in the 15th year of Amaziah (2 Ki. 14: 23), but from an assumed coreign with Jehoash which began 11 years earlier. In this way he closes up the gap of 11 years between Amaziah and Uzziah.

The prophecies of Amos are dated (Am. 1: 1 confirmed by the whole book) in a particular year, "two years before the earthquake," at a time when Jeroboam and Uzziah were both reigning. Israel has recovered from its crushed condition of the time of Hazael, and is rich and luxurious. To give time for this, the date is to be set as late as possible. The prophet dreads an invader, evidently the Assyrian, but the nation does not share his dread.

The prophecies of Hosea extend over several decades (Hos. 1: 1–2 and the whole book), the earliest being of about the same date with Amos.

THE TABLES

Foreign Dated Events.	? B. C.	Israel. Jeroboam II.	? B. C. Assyr.	Judah. Uzziah.	A. Dr.	Israelitish Dated Events.
	807	26			176	
	806	27	789 or 767	1	177	Close of interregnum. Accession of Uzziah. *Uzziah* in Judah (2 Ki. 15; 2 Chron. 26.).
	805	28		2	178	
	804	29		3	179	
	803	30		4	180	
The contemporary Assyrian history is a blank. The contemporary Egyptian history is complicated by questions of overlapping reigns.	802	31		5	181	
	801	32		6	182	
	800	33		7	183	
	799	34		8	184	
	798	35		9	185	
	797	36		10	186	
	796	37		11	187	
	795	38		12	188	
	794	39		13	189	
	793	40		14	190	? Amos.
	792	41	741*a*	15	191	? Hosea, earliest prophecies. Death of Jeroboam II.*b*
	791			16	192	Hosea's program for waiting many years without a king, and then accepting the dynasty of David (Hos. 3). Uzziah succeeds Jeroboam in the suzerainty of the region (?). ? The earthquake (Am. 1:1; Zech. 14:5).
	790			17	193	
	789			18	194	
	788			19	195	
	787			20	196	
	786			21	197	
	785			22	198	
	784			23	199	
	783			24	200	

NOTES.

a A. Di. 218. Pul is the man who later seized the throne of Assyria, and reigned as Tiglath-pilezer III. There are two mutilated Assyrian inscriptions, one of them quite long (Rawlinson's *Cuneiform Inscriptions*, Vol. 3, page 9, Nos. 2, 3, translated in Smith's *Assyrian Canon*, 117; *Assyrian Discoveries*, 275ff.; Schrader on 2 Kings 15, and other works), which mention Azariah of Judah. Of the shorter one only disconnected clauses are legible, but it speaks of populations who "to Azariah had turned and strengthened him," and of great fighting, in which of course the Assyrians defeated Azariah. The other gives details of extensive operations in northern Syria, including the punishments inflicted on wide districts that had revolted to Azariah, and including tribute from "Menahem, of Samaria" and from Damascus, Tyre, and other nationalities. These seem to be events of one campaign, and are followed by events dated in "my ninth year." Hadrach is prominently mentioned.

Assyriologists attribute these inscriptions to Tiglath-pilezer, though the events cannot be consistently placed anywhere within the 18 years of his reign. I think that they belong to the 8th year of Asshur-daan, and that Tiglath-pilezer, then an Assyrian general, had a part in them. The Canon attributes to Asshur-daan that year an expedition to Hadrach.

EXPLANATIONS OF THE DATES.

Hosea's rebukes for idolatry, lawlessness, greed, intrigue, are of course not confined to a particular date.

Jotham was 25 years old in A. Di. 229 when he began to reign (2 Ki. 15: 33).

Zechariah 6 months the 38th year of Uzziah, and Shallum 1 month in his 39th year (2 Ki. 15: 8, 13). It follows that the 6 months were at the close of the year, and the 1 at the beginning of the next year. The 39th year of Uzziah was the accession year of Menahem, and he reigned most of that year, but his 10 years were the years 40 to 49 of Uzziah (2 Ki. 15: 17, 23).

The prophesying of Isaiah extended over several decades (Isa. 1: 1 and the book), beginning in the reign of Uzziah.

Doubtless Assyrian intrigue had been many years busy in Israel, and Menahem had Assyrian support from the first. The great invasion by Pul was probably the one mentioned in the Assyrian records.

"The Burden . . . upon the land of Hadrach" is the title of the prophecy recorded in Zechariah 9–11. The name occurs nowhere else in the Bible; it is prominent in the Assyrian records of the time of Asshur-daan III and Tiglath-pilezer III. Many points in the prophecy indicate this date for it.

According to the Hebrew text, Ahaz was born 20 years before he became king in A. Di. 245 (2 Ki. 16: 2; 2 Chron. 28: 1) This would make him only 11 years old at the birth of his son Hezekiah. Some copies of the Greek substitute 25 years for 20 years, and I have followed these.

Foreign Dated Events.	? B. C.	Assyria. Shalm. III.	Israel.	? B. C. Assyr.	Judah. Uzziah.	A. Di.	Israelitish Dated Events.
? Shalmanezer III.	782	1			25	201	Hosea's program for union hindered by the idolatry and lawlessness of Israel, by the grasping spirit of Judah, and by intrigue with Egypt and Assyria (Hos. 4-6).
	781	2			26	202	
	780	3			27	203	
	779	4			28	204	
	778	5			29	205	Birth of Jotham.
	777	6			30	206	
	776	7			31	207	
	775	8			32	208	
	774	9			33	209	
? Death of Shalmanezer. Accession of Asshur-daan III. Expedition to Hadrach.	773	10			34	210	
	772	1			35	211	
	771	2			36	212	
	770	3			37	213	
	769	4		741	38	214	Zechariah, king of Israel, 6 months (2 Ki. 15:8-12).
	768	5			39	215	Shallum, 1 month (2 Ki. 15:13-16). Accession of Menahem (Hos. 7-8?). ? Leprosy of Uzziah (Zech. 11:8).
	767	6	1	741	40	216	Menahem, of Israel (2 Ki. 15: 14-22).
	766	7	2		41	217	? Isaiah, early prophecies.
Second expedition to Hadrach.	765	8	3	738	42	218	? Invasion by Pul, of Assyria. *a*
	764	9	4		43	219	? Zechariah, 9-14.
Eclipse of the sun June 15th, 10th year of Asshurdaan.	763	10	5		44	220	
	762	11	6		45	221	? Birth of Ahaz.
	761	12	7		46	222	
	760	13	8		47	223	
	759	14	9		48	224	
	758	15	10	737	49	225	Death of Menahem. Accession of Pekahiah.

NOTES.

a A. Di 227. Doubtless Assyrian intrigue was concerned with all these changes. Zechariah, of the house of Jehu, was pro-Assyrian, Shallum anti-Assyrian, Menahem and his son Pekahiah pro-Assyrian, Pekah anti-Assyrian, Hoshea at first pro-Assyrian.

b B. C. 753. The Greek and Roman dates are from the *Enclycopedia Britannica*.

c B. C. 747. For canon of Ptolemy see Introduction 8c. From this point the Babylonian chronology is continuous.

d A. Di. 243. Nowack in the *Hastings Dictionary* dates Micah perhaps 734 B. C.

e A. Di. 247. Two mutilated slabs of Tiglath-pilezer mention Pekah (Schrader, or *Assyr. Disc.*, pp. 284-286, citing from Layard page 66, and Rawlinson III, 10, 2). They speak of operations against Gaza, Egypt, Arabia, which seem to be different from those narrated in the inscriptions which describe his Philistine campaign of his 11th year (B. C. 734). They speak of Pekah being killed, but are too mutilated to tell us when or by whom. Tiglath-pilezer says that he appointed Hoshea over Israel, but not that he made him king.

Tiglath-pilezer was in Armenia in his 9th and 10th years, but the operations there were not so strenuous as to forbid the idea that he may also have operated in Palestine. Hence there is no reason for denying that the campaign occurred at the biblical date, B. C. 736. If the slabs be connected with the campaign of B. C. 734, the parts referring to Pekah may be retrospective.

In any case the interval between the death of Pekah and the final downfall of Samaria was longer than the 9 years of Hoshea. Presumably he governed as the deputy of Assyria till the death of Tiglath-pilezer, and then took upon him the state of king. This hypothesis exactly fits the biblical interim of 9 years.

EXPLANATIONS OF THE DATES.

Pekahiah's reign began the 50th year of Uzziah, and lasted 2 years (2 Ki. 15:23). Pekah the 52d year of Uzziah (2 Ki. 15:27). Hosea 9-10 fits if assigned to the time when Pekah slew Pekahiah. Isaiah 6 is dated in the year when Uzziah died.

Uzziah reigned 52 years (2 Ki. 15:2). Jotham began the second year of Pekah (2 Ki. 15:32). Jotham's regency (2 Ki. 15:5) is not counted as a part of his 16 years. It may have begun when he was a young boy (see Isa. 3:2, 12 and context).

Hezekiah was born 25 years before his first year as king, A. Di. 260 (2 Ki. 18:2).

The accounts mention here at least two invasions of Judah by Syria and Ephraim. One, begun before the death of Jotham, was successful (2 Ki. 15:37; 2 Chron. 28:1-15). In the other the Syrians captured Elath, but failed at Jerusalem (2 Ki. 16:5ff; 2 Chron. 28:23ff; Isa. 7:1ff). The Philistine and Edomite invasions (2 Chron. 28:17-18).

Jotham 16 years (2 Ki. 15:33). Ahaz 17th of Pekah (2 Ki. 16:1). Pekah smitten by Hoshea, who "reigned in his stead" the 20th year of Jotham (2 Ki. 15:30). The first year of the government of Pekah was the twentieth from the accession of Jotham.

THE TABLES

FOREIGN DATED EVENTS.	B. C.	ASSYRIA. ASSHUR-DAAN.	ISRAEL. PEKAHIAH.	? B. C. ASSYR.	JUDAH. UZZIAH.	A. Di.	ISRAELITISH DATED EVENTS.
	757	16	1	737	50	226	*Pekahiah* in Israel (2 Ki. 15: 23-27).
	756	17	2	736	51	227	Death of Pekahiah. Accession of Pekah. *a* ? Hosea 9-10.
Death of Asshur-daan III. Accession of Asshur-nirari II.	755	18	1	736	52	228	*Pekah* in Israel (2 Ki. 15 : 27ff). Death of Uzziah. Accession of Jotham as sole king (Isaiah 6).
	754	1	2	753 737	1	229	*Jotham* in Judah (2 Ki. 15:32-38; 2 Chron. 27).
Rome founded. *b*	753	2	3		2	230	
	752	3	4		3	231	
	751	4	5		4	232	
	750	5	6		5	233	
	749	6	7		6	234	
Death of Nabu-shum-ishkun. Accession of Nabonassar.	748	7	8		7	235	
Here begins the Canon of Ptolemy.*c* Nabonassar, of Babylon, 14 years.	747	8	9		8	236	Birth of Hezekiah.
	746	9	10		9	237	
Death of Asshur-nirari II. Accession of Tiglath-pilezer III, who invades Babylonia.	745	10	11		10	238	
Invades Babylonia again.	744	1	12		11	239	
Tiglath-pilezer in Arpad.	743	2	13		12	240	
Tiglath-pilezer in Arpad.	742	3	14		13	241	
Tiglath-pilezer in Arpad.	741	4	15		14	242	
Tiglath-pilezer in Arpad. About this time Piankhi and Osorkon III in Egypt. Cf. Isaiah 19.	740	5	16		15	243	? MICAH, *d* (Mic. 1:1 and book).
	739	6	17	735	16	244	Successful invasion by Rezin and Pekah. Death of Jotham. Accession of Ahaz. ODED (2 Chron. 28:9).
	738	7	18		1	245	*Ahaz* in Judah (2 Ki. 16; 2 Chron. 28; Isa. 7).
Tiglath-pilezer does desperate and protracted fighting in Media.	737	8	19		2	246	Unsuccessful invasion by Rezin and Pekah. Philistine and Edomite invasion. Ahaz tributary to Assyria.
	736	9	20	734	3	247	Deportation from the north by Tiglath-pilezer (2 Ki. 15:29). Death of Pekah. Hoshea governor. *e*
	735	10			4	248	
Tiglath-pilezer invades Philistia. Death of Nabonassar. Accession of Nadius.	734	11			5	249	? Deportation from east of Jordan by Tiglath-pilezer (1 Chron. 5:6, 26; Isa. 9:1 ?).
Nadius, of Babylon, 2 years. Tiglath-pilezer in Damascus.	733	12			6	250	

NOTES.

a A. Di. 251. More than one of the inscriptions of Tiglath-pilezer mention Ahaz among his tributaries.

b B. C. 722. Other Assyrian documents seem to date Sargon's accession 2 years later. Perhaps this is the view of the writer of 2 Kings 18: 9, who speaks of Shalmanezer as king when the siege of Samaria began. The Babylonian chronicle, however, dates the death of Shalmanezer the 10th month of his 5th year, and the accession of Sargon the 12th day of that month, and that of Merodach-baladan the following Nisan.

The records of Sargon are unusually full and well preserved, giving the events of his reign year by year ("Assyria," "Babylon," "Sargon" in the large Bible Dictionaries, or *Records of Past*, old series, vols. VII, IX, XI, or Smith, *Assyr. Disc.*, p. 288ff). Sargon was a usurper, the founder of a dynasty.

That the biblical date for the downfall of Samaria is B. C. 718, and not "about B. C. 721" (Ussher's date), any one can see by counting up the numbers. It is the fashion to say that Sargon dates that event B. C. 722, and his record is sometimes quoted in the form of a restoration based on that theory. But he says that he imposed tribute on Samaria, and that it was in arms against him 2 years later. This is explicit against this date for the final downfall.

EXPLANATIONS OF THE DATES.

The journey of Ahaz to Damascus (2 Ki. 16: 10–16; cf. 2 Chron. 28: 23; Isa. 8: 6, 9: 13, 10: 20) seems to belong to the 13th year of Tiglath-pilezer, after the Assyrians were in possession.

The later chapters of Hosea belong after Pekah, the 14th chapter contemplating perhaps the passover of Hezekiah (2 Chron. 30; cf. 2 Ki. 17: 2).

On Hoshea see note at A. Di. 247. His 9 years as king began not later than the close of the 12th year of Ahaz (2 Ki. 17: 1), and also not earlier, as the subsequent numerals show.

Hezekiah's 29 years began not later than the close of the 3d year of Hoshea (2 Ki. 18: 1, 2, 9, 10). Perhaps he was coregnant with Ahaz for a time. At all events his first year is the year that is also counted the 16th of Ahaz.

In the account of the great passover (2 Chron. 29–31) his first year is differently counted, as beginning with the Nisan after his accession.

The 3 years of the siege of Samaria (2 Ki. 18: 9, 10) are not mentioned by Sargon, but, naturally, they began in his 2d year after his defeating the allies.

Hezekiah's rebellion began when Sargon was occupied elsewhere, after the punishment of Samaria, and before Sargon's Ashdod expedition, when he speaks of Judah as in rebellion.

Probably "the 14th year of king Hezekiah" (2 Ki. 18: 13–16; Isa. 36: 1) is not an inadvertence, but the date of an earlier invasion by Sennacherib. It is not likely that Sargon, after reducing Ashdod, left Judah wholly unpunished. Probably he sent an army the following year under his son Sennacherib against Hezekiah.

Hezekiah's sickness is dated that same 14th year—15 years before the close of his 29 years (2 Ki. 20: 6).

THE TABLES

Foreign Dated Events.	B. C.	Assyria. Tig. Pil. III.	Israel. Hoshea.	? B. C. Assyr.	Judah. Ahaz.	A. Di.	Israelitish Dated Events.
Tiglath-pilezer in Damascus. Death of Nadius, of Babylon. Accession of Yukin-zer, 3 years.	732	13			7	251	? Ahaz meets Tiglath-pilezer in Damascus. *a*
	731	14			8	252	
	730	15			9	253	
Tiglath-pilezer captures Yukin-zer, and becomes king of Babylon for 2 years; the Porus of Ptolemy.	729	16			10	254	? Hosea 11–13.
	728	17			11	255	
Death of Tiglath-pilezer. Accession of Shalmanezer IV over Assyria and Babylon for 5 years. The Ilulaeus of Ptolemy.	727	18			12	256	
	726	1	1	734	13	257	Hoshea becomes king (2 Ki. 15:30, 17:1-18:12).
	725	2	2		14	258	
	724	3	3		15	259	
	723	4	4	726 or 715	16 1	260	Isaiah 14:28ff. Death of Ahaz. Accession and 1st year of Hezekiah.
Death of Shalmanezer. Accession of Sargon in Assyria. He captures Samaria and imposes tribute. *b* Merodachbaladan in Babylon for 12 years.	722	5	5		2	261	Great passover. Hezekiah (2 Ki. 18–20; Isa. 36-39; 2 Chron. 29-32).
	721	1	6		3	262	
Sargon defeats Shabaka of Egypt with Samaria and other allies. Fights Ummanigas of Elam.	720	2	7		4	263	Final siege of Samaria begun.
	719	3	8		5	264	
	718	4	9	722	6	265	? 65 years (Isa. 7:8). Final downfall of Samaria.
From his 2d to his 10th years Sargon was fighting Merodach-baladan, the Elamites, the Medes, Armenia, etc., in many cases deporting the inhabitants to the regions east of the Mediterranean.	717	5			7	266	
	716	6			8	267	? Hezekiah rebels against Assyria. ? Smites the Philistines.
	715	7			9	268	
	714	8			10	269	
	713	9			11	270	
	712	10			12	271	
Sargon's expedition to Ashdod.	711	11			13	272	Isaiah 20.
? Sargon "subjugator of Judah." Sargon captures Merodach-baladan, and becomes king of Babylon for 5 years.	710	12			14	273	First invasion by Sennacherib. Hezekiah's sickness. Ambassadors from Merodach-baladan.
	709	13			15	274	
	708	14			16	275	

NOTES.

a B. C. 705. Ptolemy describes these 2 years of Sennacherib as an interregnum.

b A. Di. 282. The Bible says that Sennacherib purposed to deport the whole population; his failing of this was a victory for Judah, though only a remnant remained (2 Ki. 18: 32, 19: 29–31). "That night" (2 Ki. 19: 35) is the night when Jehovah fulfilled his threat, not necessarily the night after the prophet uttered the threat. There is nothing in the Bible to contradict Sennacherib's statement that he left Palestine a victor, and that Hezekiah sent tribute after him.

c B. C. 700, 698. The Babylonians carried away their gods in ships across the Persian Gulf. Two years later Sennacherib brought the gods back. Note how exactly the passages in Isaiah fit if they are regarded as allusions to these events.

d B. C. 697. This is the one record of a great reverse found in the Assyrian annals (Taylor cylinder, and Nebbi-Yunus inscription). Sennacherib does not say how many of his men perished. But he had to return at once to Nineveh. One can imagine the sensation produced in Judah when the tidings reached there. Why should not the prophet, when he came to write of Jehovah's providences in the matter of Sennacherib, recall these successive events in which Jehovah protected his people by his dealings with the other nations?

e B. C. 688. Ptolemy counts these 8 years an interregnum.

EXPLANATIONS OF THE DATES.

Supplemented from the records of Sennacherib and from other sources, the Assyrian numbers here given are from the Eponym Canon (see Introduction 10); the Babylonian numbers are those of the Canon of Ptolemy (Introduction 8) and the Babylonian list of kings. I have used the Babylonian names, but have omitted some of the shorter reigns. For the Babylonian lists see *Records of the Past*, new series I; for Sennacherib see same VI and IV, and old series I, VII, IX, XI.

Manasseh began to reign at 12 years of age (2 Ki. 21: 1).

The great invasion by Sennacherib (2 Ki. 18: 17ff; Isa. 36: 2ff) was not the one in Hezekiah's 14th year (2 Ki. 18: 13–16; Isa. 36: 1); the Assyrian records date it in the 4th year of Sennacherib.

The details of the withdrawal of Sennacherib were of such a nature that agriculture was not resumed till the third year (2 Ki. 19: 29). Therefore, the annihilation of Sennacherib's army was not an event which occurred at once there in Palestine. The processes by which Jehovah, king of nations, saved Judah are those which appear in the left-hand column of the table.

Hezekiah reigned 29 years (2 Ki. 18: 2).

THE TABLES

Foreign Dated Events.	B. C.	Babylon. Sargon.	Assyria. Sargon.	Judah. Hezekiah.	A. Di.	Israelitish Dated Events.
Third year of Sargon in Babylon.	707	3	15	17	276	
	706	4	16	18	277	Birth of Manasseh.
Death of Sargon. Accession of Sennacherib in Assyria and Babylon. *a*	705	5	17	19	278	
Sennacherib fighting with Merodach-baladan.	704	1	1	20	279	
Sennacherib makes Belibni king in Babylon.	703	2	2	21	280	
	702	1	3	22	281	
Sennacherib invades Palestine. Tirhakah in Egypt (2 Ki. 18:21, 19:9).	701	2	4	23	282	Judah invaded by Sennacherib.*b*
Sennacherib invades Babylonia. The gods flee to Elam.*c* He makes his son, Asshur-nadin-shuma, king.	700	3	5	24	283	? Isaiah 43:14, 46:1-2.
	699	1	6	25	284	Agriculture resumed in Judah.
Fights Babylon and Elam and brings back the fugitive gods.	698	2	7	26	285	
Fighting Elam. His army crushed by a winter storm.*d*	697	3	8	27	286	? The 185,000 (2 Ki. 19:35 and parallels).
Fighting in Elam and Babylonia.	696	4	9	28	287	
	695	5	10	29	288	Death of Hezekiah. Accession of Manasseh.
Elamites dethrone Asshur-nadin-shuma.	694	6	11	1	289	*Manasseh* of Judah (2 Ki. 21; 2 Chron. 33).
Sennacherib devastates Elam and Babylonia Nergal-ushezib, 1 year.	693	1	12	2	290	
Mushezib-marduk, 4 years.	692	1	13	3	291	
Sennacherib defeats Elam and Babylon at Hhalule.	691	2	14	4	292	
	690	3	15	5	293	
In November, Sennacherib sacks and nearly destroys Babylon.	689	4	16	6	294	? Isaiah 47, 48:20.
Sennacherib in Babylon 8 years. *e*	688	1	17	7	295	
	687	2	18	8	296	
	686	3	19	9	297	
Second Messenian war, B. C. 685-668.	685	4	20	10	298	
Archonship at Athens made annual.	684	5	21	11	299	
	683	6	22	12	300	

Notes.

a B. C. 674. These accounts of the migrations of the gods are pretty frequent in the Assyrian and Babylonian records.

b B. C. 668. Asshurbanipal and Shamash-shum-ukin were sons of Esarhaddon. The Babylonian chronicle assigns but 12 years to Esarhaddon, and gives particulars. For chronological convenience, however, I have followed Ptolemy, giving him 13 years.

Explanations of the Dates.

The column of Foreign Dated Events is made up from the Babylonian Chronicle (*Rec. of Past*, new series I) or from the records of Esarhaddon or Asshurbanipal. The originals often date the events by the month and the day.

We can only conjecture the date when Manasseh began to persecute the prophets. Presumably the change from the policy of Hezekiah was gradual. There is no difficulty in the way of conjecturing that Isaiah may have lived long enough to have heard the news of the death of Sennacherib, and to have written Isaiah 37: 38 (cf. 2 Chron. 32: 32).

Amon was born 22 years before he became king (2 Ki. 21: 19). See A. Di. 344.

FOREIGN DATED EVENTS.	B. C.	BABYLON. SENNACHERIB.	ASSYRIA. SENNACHERIB.	JUDAH. MANASSEH.	A. DI.	ISRAELITISH DATED EVENTS.
	682	7	23	13	301	
Death of Sennacherib. Accession of Esarhaddon.	681	8	24	14	302	
	680	1	1	15	303	? Manasseh persecuting the prophets.
Early in his reign he operates against Sidon, and claims Judah and all the neighboring kings as tributary.	679	2	2	16	304	? Death of Isaiah.
	678	3	3	17	305	
	677	4	4	18	306	
Sidon subdued.	676	5	5	19	307	
Esarhaddon in Egypt.	675	6	6	20	308	
Esarhaddon in Egypt. The gods of Accad move from Elam to the city of Accad. *a*	674	7	7	21	309	
	673	8	8	22	310	
	672	9	9	23	311	
Severe and decisive fighting in Egypt.	671	10	10	24	312	
	670	11	11	25	313	
	669	12	12	26	314	
Death of Esarhaddon. Accession of Asshurbanipal in Assyria and Shamash-shum-ukin in Babylon. *b* Asshurbanipal at once invaded Egypt, taking tribute from Judah and 22 other kingdoms on the way.	668	13	13	27	315	
	667	1	1	28	316	
	666	2	2	29	317	
	665	3	3	30	318	
Death of Tirhakah (Apis-stele, Schrader on Nah. 3:8).	664	4	4	31	319	
Sack of Thebes by Asshurbanipal.	663	5	5	32	320	
	662	6	6	33	321	
	661	7	7	34	322	
	660	8	8	35	323	Birth of Amon.
Founding of Byzantium.	659	9	9	36	324	
	658	10	10	37	325	

Notes.

a A. Di. 336. Nahum threatens the overthrow of Assyria. Zephaniah does the same. Apparently, Assyria had never been so prosperous as under Asshurbanipal. His dominion extended from Egypt to the far east. But it was a prosperity produced by the overstraining of resources in holding peoples in subjection by brute force. Perhaps Nahum and Zephaniah had the sagacity to recognize its fictitious character. The collapse, when it came, was sudden and complete.

Explanations of the Dates.

It is a plausible conjecture that the generals of the Assyrian king carried Manasseh to Babylon (2 Chron. 33: 11) at the time when Asshurbanipal was besieging the city. That leaves but a few years of his old age for the reformation (2 Chron. 33: 13ff) that followed his return.

It is believed that Nahum prophesied for the generation that witnessed the sack of Thebes by Asshurbanipal B. C. 663 (Nah. 3: 8). Also he seems to have prophesied during a period of reform in Judah (1: 15).

Josiah was 8 years old when he began to reign (2 Ki. 22: 1), 345 A. Di.

Manasseh reigned 55 years (2 Ki. 21: 1). Amon reigned 2 years (2 Ki. 21: 19). The actual time might be a year more or a year less than that assigned in the table. The mean number is safest, and is confirmed by the long number at 362 A. Di.

Zephaniah is dated in the reign of Josiah (1: 1), following a reformation from which some have apostatized (1: 4ff). This was the reformation of the last years of Manasseh, rather than that of the 18th year of Josiah

THE TABLES

Foreign Dated Events.	B. C.	Babylon. Shamash-shum-ukin.	Assyria. Asshurbanipal.	Judah. Manasseh.	A. Di.	Israelitish Dated Events.
	657	11	11	38	326	
	656	12	12	39	327	
In these years Shamash-shum-ukin was stirring up the peoples everywhere against Asshurbanipal.	655	13	13	40	328	
	654	14	14	41	329	
	653	15	15	42	330	
	652	16	16	43	331	
	651	17	17	44	332	
	650	18	18	45	333	
	649	19	19	46	334	
Asshurbanipal captures Babylon. Shamash-shum-ukin dies by fire. He was followed in Babylon by Isiniladanus, who is, perhaps, Asshurbanipal under another name. In the years following the capture of Babylon, Asshurbanipal took vengeance on the allies of his brother, including the seacoast.	648	20	20	47	335	? Manasseh carried to Babylon.
	647	1	21	48	336	? His return and reformation. ? NAHUM. *a*
	646	2	22	49	337	Birth of Josiah.
	645	3	23	50	338	
	644	4	24	51	339	
	643	5	25	52	340	
	642	6	26	53	341	
	641	7	27	54	342	
Asshurbanipal captures Susa, and puts an end to the kingdom of Elam. (Hommel on "Assyria" in *Dic. of the Bib.*).	640	8	28	55	343	Manasseh dies. Amon succeeds him.
	639	9	29	1	344	*Amon*, king of Judah (2 Ki. 21:19-26; 2 Chron. 33:21-25).
	638	10	30	2/1	345	Death of Amon. Accession of Josiah. *Josiah*, king of Judah (2 Ki. 22-23; 2 Chron. 34-35).
	637	11	31	2	346	
	636	12	32	3	347	? ZEPHANIAH.
	635	13	33	4	348	
	634	14	34	5	349	
	633	15	35	6	350	

NOTES.

a B. C. 632. These Scythian invaders appear in the inscriptions as "Manda." It is not in all cases easy to avoid confusing them with the Medes. Apparently there has been an element of confusion from the time of Herodotus.

b A. Di. 369. Our copies of Chronicles date this birth 10 years later (2 Chron. 36: 9).

c A. Di. 375. The Bible is doubtless correct in saying that Neco was marching against the king of Assyria, Josiah's suzerain. Josephus (*Ant.* X, v, 1) is partly right in saying that the march was against the Medes and Babylonians. The Assyrian was moribund, and the question was which of the rival powers could seize upon the estate.

EXPLANATIONS OF THE DATES.

In his 8th year Josiah began to "seek after the God of David his father," and he began to "purge Judah" in his 12th year (2 Chron. 34: 3).

Jehoiakim was 25 years old, and Jehoahaz 23 years old, when they each began to reign, A. Di. 376 (2 Ki. 23: 36, 31).

Jeremiah began prophesying the 13th year of Josiah (Jer. 1: 2, 25: 3, 1).

The date in the 18th year of Josiah (2 Ki. 22: 3, 23: 23; 2 Chron. 34: 8, 35: 19) is that of the great passover, which began the middle of the first month of the year. It follows that a good many of the events that are mentioned occurred the preceding year.

Josephus says (*Ant.* X, iv, 4) that Josiah's profanation of the altar at Bethel (2 Ki. 23: 15ff) occurred 361 years after it was foretold by Jadon (see 1 Ki. 13). Apparently this is in Josephus a genuine traditional number. It disagrees with most of the chronological schemes that have been framed. It fits accurately the chronology of these tables, and is a confirmation of no small value.

Zedekiah was born 21 years before his first year, A. Di. 387; and Jehoiachin 18 years before he occupied the throne in A. Di. 386 (2 Ki. 24: 18, 8).

The death of Josiah occurred in the 31st year of his reign. That was the year of the Neco expedition. The 3 months of Jehoahaz may have been in that year, or in the year following (2 Ki. 22: 1, 23: 29ff).

THE TABLES

Foreign Dated Events.	B. C.	Babylon. Isiniladanus.	Assyria. Asshurbanipal.	Judah. Josiah.	A. Di.	Israelitish Dated Events.
About this time, according to the Greek historians, the Assyrian empire invaded by a people whom they call Scythians, the field of the invasion extending from the far east to the Mediterranean. *a*	632	16	36	7	351	
	631	17	37	8	352	Josiah begins to seek after God. Jehoiakim born.
	630	18	38	9	353	
	629	19	39	10	354	Jehoahaz born.
	628	20	40	11	355	
	627	21	41	12	356	Josiah begins his reforms,
Death of Isiniladanus. Accession of Nabopolassar.	626	22	42	13	357	JEREMIAH begins prophesying.
First year of Nabopolassar.	625	1		14	358	
Legislation of Draco at Athens.	624	2	History of Assyria fragmentary till its downfall, B. C. 607.	15	359	
	623	3		16	360	
	622	4		17	361	Josiah's great reformation.
	621	5		18	362	The reformation passover. HULDAH (2 Ki. 22:14). 361 years after Jadon.
	620	6		19	363	
	619	7		20	364	
	618	8		21	365	
	617	9		22	366	
	616	10		23	367	Birth of Zedekiah.
	615	11		24	368	
	614	12		25	369	Birth of Jehoiachin. *b*
	613	13		26	370	
	612	14		27	371	
	611	15		28	372	
	610	16		29	373	
	609	17		30	374	
	608	18		31	375	Expedition of Pharaoh-Neco. *c* Death of Josiah. *Jehoahaz* 3 months.

NOTES.

a A. Di. 377. A dominant note in Habakkuk is dread of the Chaldæans, who are overrunning the earth. Perhaps the time of Nabopolassar, after the overthrow of Nineveh.

b A. Di. 390. Ezekiel began prophesying the 5th day of the 4th month of a year described as "the 30th year," and as "the 5th year of king Jehoiachin's captivity" (Ezek. 1:1-2). It may have been the 30th year of the prophet's age, or from Josiah's great reform year. The era of the "captivity" is mentioned five times in the Bible (2 Ki. 25:27; Jer. 52:31; Ezek. 1:2, 33:21, 40:1). Its first year is the 11th of Jehoiakim, the year when Jehoiachin and the best of the people were deported. Most or all of the other dates in Ezekiel are in terms of the years of Zedekiah, the first year of Zedekiah being one year later than the first year of the "captivity."

c A. Di. 390 and 397. This is the proper place for looking at certain long numbers, found in the Bible and Josephus, for the times of the kings. We take them in their order.

Josephus says that the downfall of

(Continued on page 158.)

EXPLANATIONS OF THE DATES.

The date of Jehoiakim's submission (2 Ki. 24:1) must be that when Daniel was carried to Babylon (Dan. 1:1), the accession year of Nebuchadnezzar, not his first year.

Baruch's reading of Jeremiah's prophecies is dated in the 4th and 5th years of Jehoiakim (Jer. 36:1, 9). The 3 years (2 Ki. 24:1) of Jehoiakim's fidelity to Nebuchadnezzar were his 3d, 4th and 5th years—Nebuchadnezzar's accession year, his first year, and his 2d year. The same were the 3 years (Dan. 1:5) of the training of Daniel and his companions. Nebuchadnezzar's dream occurred before the close of the 3d of these 3 years (Dan. 2:1).

Jehoiakim 11 years (2 Ki. 23:36). Jehoiachin deported in the 8th year of Nebuchadnezzar (2 Ki. 24:12).

For the date when Ezekiel began to prophesy see Note *b*. The Hananiah incident the 4th year of Zedekiah (Jer. 28:1 and marg. of 27:1).

Ezekiel 8:1 gives the date the 5th day of the 6th month of the 6th year, and Ezekiel 20:1 the 10th day of the 5th month of the 7th year.

For the date of the investment of Jerusalem see 2 Kings 25:1; Ezekiel 24:1. For details see 2 Kings 25; 2 Chronicles 36; Jeremiah 39, 52; Ezekiel 24-39.

The events of the year A. Di. 396 are Jeremiah's purchase of land (Jer. 32; cf. 33-34), dated the 10th year of Zedekiah "which was the 18th year of Nebuchadnezzar" (Jer. 32:1); Egyptian interference (Jer. 37-38; cf. Ezekiel's prophecies against Egypt); the incident of the fiery furnace (Dan. 3) according to some copies of the Septuagint; the deportation of 832 persons (18th of Nebuchadnezzar, Jer. 52:29); Ezekiel's denunciation of Egypt (Ezek. 29-30), the 12th day of the 10th month (29:1).

The date in Ezekiel 26:1 is the first day of some month of the 11th year; in 31:1 it is the first day of the 3d month of the 11th year. For the taking of Jerusalem see 2 Kings 24:18, 25:8, etc. Ezekiel got the details from a fugitive 5 months later, in the 12th year of "our captivity" (Ezek. 33:21). The 12th year in Ezekiel 32:1, 17 may be that of "our captivity."

THE TABLES

Foreign Dated Events.	B. C.	Babylon. Nabopolassar.	Judah.	Judah. Jehoiakim.	A. Di.	Israelitish Dated Events.
Downfall of Nineveh.	607	19		1	376	*Jehoiakim* (2 Ki. 23 : 34-24 : 7 and 2 Chron. and Jer.).
	606	20		2	377	? HABAKKUK. *a*
Death of Nabopolassar. Accession of Nebuchadnezzar.	605	21		3	378	Jehoiakim submits to Nebuchadnezzar. DANIEL taken into exile (Dan. 1).
First year of Nebuchadnezzar. He defeats Egypt in the great battle of Carchemish, and becomes sovereign of the east.	604	1		4	379	? URIAH son of Shemaiah (Jer. 26 : 20ff). BARUCH (Jer. 36, 45).
	603	2	Years of the "Captivity."	5	380	{ Baruch, 9th month (Jer. 36). Jehoiakim rebels. Daniel expounds the king's dream (Dan. 2).
	602	3		6	381	
	601	4		7	382	
	600	5		8	383	Jehoiakim reduced by Nebuchadnezzar (Jos. *Ant.* X, vi, 1). ? Jonadab (Jer. 35).
	599	6		9	384	
	598	7		10	385	3023 deported 7th year of Nebuchadnezzar (Jer. 52 : 28).
	597	8	1	11	386	Death of Jehoiakim. *Jehoiachin* 3 months. The great deportation. Accession of Zedekiah.
	596	9	2	1	387	*Zedekiah* (2 Ki. 24-25; Chron.; Jer.; Ezek.). ? Jeremiah and the figs (24).
	595	10	3	2	388	? Jeremiah to the exiles (29; cf. 30-31). ? Jeremiah against Elam (49 : 34ff).
Legislation of Solon at Athens.	594	11	4	3	389	{ EZEKIEL prophesying (1-7). *b* 390 years (Ezek. 4 : 5). *c* Jeremiah and Hananiah (Jer. 27-28). Jeremiah against Babylon (Jer. 50-51). Zedekiah goes to Babylon (Jer. 51 : 59).
	593	12	5	4	390	
	592	13	6	5	391	
	591	14	7	6	392	Zedekiah's perjury (Ezek. 8-19, espec. 17 : 11ff).
	590	15	8	7	393	Ezekiel 20-23.
	589	16	9	8	394	
Pythian games begun.	588	17	10	9	395	Jerusalem invested 10th day of 10th month.
	587	18	11	10	396	[For events see opposite page.]
	586	19	12	11	397	{ Ezekiel against Tyre (26-28). Ezekiel against Egypt (31). Jerusalem burned 7th day of 5th month. Zedekiah 11 years (2 Ki. 24 : 18). Gedaliah. Flight to Egypt (Jer. 40-44). When Ezekiel hears the news (33-39).
Nebuchadnezzar lays siege to Tyre for many years.	585	20	13		398	
	584	21	14		399	
	583	22	15		400	Ezekiel against Egypt (32).

NOTES.

(Continued from page 156.)

Samaria occurred 240 years, 7 months and 7 days after the disruption (*Ant.* IX, xiv, 1). Evidently this number is obtained by adding the regnal numbers of the books of kings, counting Joram's reign (2 Ki. 9:29) as eleven years. The 7 months and 7 days are the reigns of Zechariah, Shallum, and Zimri. It has value as indicating that the numbers have been correctly transmitted, but no other value, inasmuch as it interprets the numbers falsely, and neglects the interregna.

EXPLANATIONS OF THE DATES.

The date given in Ezekiel 40:1 is the 25th year of "our captivity;" "14 years after that the city was smitten," the 10th day of the year.

Ezekiel promised Egypt to Nebuchadnezzar the 27th year, presumably of Zedekiah, possibly of "our captivity."

Our knowledge of Nebuchadnezzar's invading Egypt in his 37th year comes from an inscription.

"In yet 65 years Ephraim shall be broken that it be not a people" (Isa. 7:8). This number has thus far proved a hopeless puzzle. It agrees with our tables if we regard it as affirming that the downfall of Samaria will occur in the year '65 of the disruption, '65 being put by abbreviation for 265.

The statement of Josephus (see at A. Di. 362) that Jadon's prediction was fulfilled 361 years after it was made agrees exactly with these tables, though it is in conflict with other statements of Josephus.

The 390 of Ezekiel 4:5 coincides with the number of the years from the disruption. It is less easy to match this with a coincidence for the 40 of Ezekiel 4:6.

Josephus incorrectly says (*Ant.* X, viii, 5 and ix, 7) that the destruction of Jerusalem occurred the 18th year of Nebuchadnezzar. He says that this was 130 years, 6 months, 10 days after the carrying away of the ten tribes. Now 265 plus $130\frac{1}{2}$ equals $395\frac{1}{2}$, the middle of the 18th year of Nebuchadnezzar as given in the table (*Ant.* X, ix, 7).

He says (*Ant.* X, viii, 5) that the temple was destroyed 470 years, 6 months, 10 days after it was built. He says that Solomon reigned 80 years (*Ant.* VIII, vii, 8), that is, 76 years after the founding of the temple in his 4th year. Add 76 to $395\frac{1}{2}$ and we have $470\frac{1}{2}$ within one year.

He says (*Ant.* X, viii, 4) that David's dynasty lasted $514\frac{1}{2}$ years. To the $470\frac{1}{2}$ add 40 years of David and Solomon's 4 years before founding the temple, and you have the $514\frac{1}{2}$. Compare Josephus *Ant.* XI, iv, 8, some copies, and VI, xiv, 9. Apparently Josephus takes this 514 years, 6 months, 10 days of the dynasty of David, and, by carelessly adding 18, obtains 532 years, 6 months, 10 days for the whole period of monarchy.

The argument from these long numbers in confirmation of my chronology does not depend on the trustworthiness of Josephus, but on the coincidences presented. These would be virtually impossible unless the coinciding numbers were correct.

THE TABLES

FOREIGN DATED EVENTS.	B. C.	BABYLONIA. NEBUCHADNEZ-ZAR.	"Our captivity."	A. Di.	ISRAELITISH DATED EVENTS.
Josephus says (*Ant.* X, ix, 7) that Nebuchadnezzar invaded Egypt.	582	23	16	401	745 deported (Jer. 52:30).
	581	24	17	402	
	580	25	18	403	
	579	26	19	404	
	578	27	20	405	
	577	28	21	406	
	576	29	22	407	
	575	30	23	408	
Æsop, sixth century B. C.	574	31	24	409	
	573	32	25	410	Ezekiel 40–48.
	572	33	26	411	
	571	34	27	412	
	570	35	28	413	Ezekiel promises Egypt to Nebuchadnezzar, first month, first day (Ezek. 29:17).
	569	36	29	414	
Nebuchadnezzar invades Egypt.	568	37	30	415	
	567	38	31	416	
	566	39	32	417	
	565	40	33	418	
	564	41	34	419	
	563	42	35	420	
Death of Nebuchadnezzar. Accession of Evil-merodach.	562	43	36	421	
	561	1	37	422	Jehoiachin released 25th day of 12th month (2 Ki. 25:27-30; Jer. 52:31-34).
Pisistratus tyrant of Athens till B. C. 527. Death of Evil-merodach. Accession of Neriglissar.	560	2		423	
	559	1		424	
	558	2		425	

Notes.

a B. C. 539. At this point the Bible brings in "Darius the Mede" (Dan. 5:31, 6:1, 6, 9, 25, 28, 9:1, 11:1). The original makes Daniel 5:31 the opening of the following story, not the close of the preceding story. There is no implication that the accession of Darius was connected with the slaying of Belshazzar, and this idea should be eliminated as misleading.

This Darius is not mentioned under this name in any known literature outside the Bible. He has been identified with various persons, for example with Astyages or with Cyaxares, kings of Media, or with Gobryas, the general of Cyrus, who captured Babylon, or with the later king, Darius Hystaspis. As plausible a notion as any is that Darius is Cyrus himself under another name.

For most purposes, however, we have no need to solve this problem. At all events the first year of this Darius is the first year of Cyrus; and this is sufficient for adjusting the dates.

Explanations of the Dates.

The dated events for Cyrus are taken from inscriptions of Nabonidus and Cyrus, which give the dates in years of the reign of Nabonidus (e. g. *Rec. of Past*, new ser. V).

The Persian-Babylonian accounts mention Belshazzar, but the dates for him in these tables are from the Bible. The third year of Belshazzar Daniel was in Shushan on the king's business (Dan. 8:1, 2, 27). It follows that this was after Daniel entered the service of the Persian king, and therefore after the taking of Babylon by Cyrus; and that the third year of Belshazzar was his last year; and therefore that his three years were the years 15, 16, 17 of Nabonidus.

Daniel's counting this date in terms of the years of Belshazzar (not those of the Persian king) is paralleled by the Cyrus inscription, which counts his exploits in terms of the years of Nabonidus.

Daniel's vision of the four beasts is dated the first year of Belshazzar, and his next vision the third year of Belshazzar (Dan. 7:1, 8:1). The fourth month of this year the generals of Cyrus captured Babylon. Belshazzar's feast probably occurred earlier. In the succeeding months Daniel received rapid promotion (Dan. 8:2, 27, 6:1-4). The affair of the lions probably belongs to the same year, or early the following year. In that following year, the first year of Darius and of Cyrus (Dan. 9:1, and see note), Daniel was concerned for the restoration of Jerusalem (Dan. 9). He now had great prestige and influence. Presumably it was due to this that the first returning exiles reached Jerusalem this year, early enough to set up the altar in the seventh month (Ezra 1 and 3).

Daniel's last vision is dated the third year of Cyrus (Dan. 10:1). He probably died soon after, and his death enabled the opponents of the Jews to make headway at court.

THE TABLES

Foreign Dated Events.	B. C.	Babylon. Neriglissar.	A. Di.	Israelitish Dated Events.
	557	3	426	
Death of Neriglissar. Accession of Nabonidus. First mention of Cyrus, king of Anshan (Shushan).	556	4	427	
	555	1	428	
Cyrus making headway against the Manda.	554	2	429	
	553	3	430	
	552	4	431	
	551	5	432	
	550	6	433	
Cyrus has become king of the Medes.	549	7	434	
? Cyrus conquers Croesus.	548	8	435	
Cyrus is called king of Persia.	547	9	436	
	546	10	437	
	545	11	438	
	544	12	439	
	543	13	440	
	542	14	441	
Belshazzar reigns with Nabonidus.	541	15	442	Daniel's vision of lion, bear, leopard and fourth beast (Dan. 7).
? Pythagoras flor. B. C. 540-510.	540	16	443	
Babylon taken by Gobryas, July. Babylon occupied by Cyrus, October. *a*	539	17	444	Belshazzar's feast (Dan. 5). Daniel in the Persian service. Daniel's vision of ram, he-goat, etc. (Dan. 8).
Cyrus king in Babylon, first year.	538	1	445	? Daniel in the den of lions (Dan. 6). Daniel's prayer for Jerusalem (Dan. 9). The decree for the return (Ezra 1). The altar set up, 7th month (Ezra 3: 1-6).
	537	2	446	Temple founded, second month (Ezra 3).
Polycrates tyrant of Samos cir. B. C. 536-522.	536	3	447	Daniel's last vision (Dan. 10-12).
? Thespis first exhibits tragedy.	535	4	448	The building of the temple hindered for many years (Ezra 4).
	534	5	449	Jeshua high priest from before the first year of Cyrus.
	533	6	450	

NOTES.

a B. C. 531. Cyrus had a "first year" as king of Anshan before B. C. 556; and a "first year" as king of the Medes and Persians about B. C. 550. His first year as "king of kings" was B. C. 538. If "Darius the Mede" was his associate, Cyrus may have had yet another "first year," when he became sole king. Cambyses was coregnant with Cyrus during more or less of the nine years of his reign as king of kings.

b A. Di. 461. The narrative in Ezra mentions two Persian kings between Cyrus and Darius Hystaspis, calling them Ahasuerus and Artaxerxes. The natural suggestion is that they are the two who actually came in that order, and who are commonly known as Cambyses and Gomates. The difference in the names is not an insuperable objection, since it is common for a king to be known by two or more names. The opposing view to the effect that these two kings are the later Xerxes and Artaxerxes introduces inextricable confusion into the narrative.

To understand the matter one should read carefully the Persian account of the events as found in the Greek historians and in the great Behistun inscription of Darius. See books of reference, including *Rec. of Past*, old series, I and VII. Darius emphasizes his reversing the policy of Gomates, who had reversed the policy of his Achemenian predecessors. This fits the biblical account. It fits also the fact that they resumed the work without asking permission, claiming that the stopping of it had been a nullity (Ezra 5: 16).

In the first six years of his reign Darius claims to have overthrown at least nine usurpers, fighting about twenty great battles, most of which he dates by the month and the day. The books of Ezra and Haggai and Zechariah should be read in the light of these facts of the history.

EXPLANATIONS OF THE DATES.

After the death of Daniel the opponents of the Jews were successful in lobbying against them at the Persian court, hindering their plans during the rest of the reign of Cyrus and the eight years of Cambyses (called Ahasuerus in Ezra). Their opposition was doubtless the more effective because of the unsettled condition of things in Palestine due to the war of Cambyses against Egypt.

Great changes occurred near the close of the seventh year of Cambyses. The Persian dates in the table are from the Behistun inscription (see Note *b*), and numerical dates appear in Ezra 4: 24; Haggai 1: 1, 15, 2: 1, 10, 20; Zechariah 1: 1, 7, 7: 1. A close examination of the Persian and the biblical dated events shows that they dovetail into one another most remarkably.

The usurper variously known as Gomates, Bardes, pseudo-Smerdis, is not recognized in Ptolemy's canon, and his reign may have been counted as a nullity by his successors. But he was actually on the throne during parts of two calendar years, about seven months in all. This agrees with the statement in I Esdras 5: 73, to the effect that the work on the temple was suspended two years.

The completion of the temple was in the vernal year corresponding with B. C. 516, but actually in February of B. C. 515.

Foreign Dated Events.	B.C.	Persia. Cyrus.	A. Di.	Israelitish Dated Events.
	532	7	451	Temple work still hindered (Ezra 4).
Cambyses coregnant with Cyrus. *a*	531	8	452	
Death of Cyrus. Accession of Cambyses.	530	9	453	
First year of Cambyses.	529	1	454	
	528	2	455	
	527	3	456	
	526	4	457	
Cambyses conquers Egypt.	525	5	458	
	524	6	459	
Gomates rose up 12th mo., 14th day.	523	7	460	
He became king 5th mo., 9th day.	522	8	461	Work on temple suspended (Ezra 4:7-24). *b*
Gomates slain 1st mo., 10th day. Darius king. Revolts crushed in Susiana, Babylonia, Media, 9th mo., 27th day, and 10th mo., 2d and 27th days.	521	1	462	HAGGAI prophesies 6th mo., 1st day. Work on temple 6th mo., 24th day. Interference of Tattenai (Ezra 5). Haggai 7th mo. (2:1-9).
Revolt crushed in Armenia, 2d, 3d and 10th months.	520	2	463	ZECHARIAH 8th mo. (1:1-6). Haggai 9th mo. (2:10-23). Zechariah 11th mo. (1:7-6:15). Favorable reply of Darius (Ezra 6).
Revolts crushed in Armenia, Media, Sagartia, Parthia, 2d, 4th and 12th months.	519	3	464	
Revolt in Parthia crushed 5th month. Revolt in Margiana crushed 9th month.	518	4	465	Zechariah, Chaps. 7-8.
Revolt crushed in Persia, 2d, 5th, 10th and 12th months.	517	5	466	
Revolt crushed in Babylonia, 8th month.	516	6	467	Temple finished 3d of Adar (Ezra 6:15ff).
Anacreon in Athens from B. C. 522.	515	7	468	Passover (Ezra 6:19-22).
	514	8	469	For nearly 60 years from this time we have no direct information concerning the Jews in Palestine.
	513	9	470	
	512	10	471	Jeshua still high priest.
	511	11	472	
	510	12	473	
Tarquin expelled from Rome. First treaty of Rome with Carthage.	509	13	474	
	508	14	475	

NOTES.

a B. C. 485. Xerxes is simply a modified form of the name which appears in the Bible as Ahasuerus.

Josephus, following some copies of the Septuagint, places the activities of Ezra and Nehemiah in the time of Xerxes, and the events of the book of Esther in the time of his successor, Artaxerxes. Several considerations show that this is erroneous, and that our common Hebrew text is correct. For the king of Ezra and Nehemiah the Bible gives a date in his thirty-second year, and Josephus gives dates in his twenty-fifth and twenty-eighth years (Neh. 5: 14, 13:6; Jos. *Ant.* XI, v, 7, 8), while Xerxes reigned only 21 years. Add to this the interfitting of the Persian and the biblical events, as exhibited in the table.

EXPLANATIONS OF THE DATES.

The three first high priests after the exile were Jeshua, who held the office in B. C. 538 (Ezra 3: 2, etc.), Eliashib, who held it B. C. 444 to 433 (Neh. 3: 1, 20, 21 and 13: 4), and Joiakim (Neh. 12: 10, 12, 26), who came between the two. Because the time is so long we infer that Jeshua's term began not long before B. C. 538, and that Eliashib's term closed not long after B. C. 433. For other facts bearing in the same direction see under Johanan at page 173. On the basis of these data the approximate dates of the first three high priests are obtained for the table by averaging.

The deposition of Vashti is dated in the third year of Xerxes (Esth. 1: 3).

Foreign Dated Events.	B. C.	Persia. Dar. Hys.	A. Di.	Israelitish Dated Events.
About this time Darius conquered Thrace and Macedonia.	507	15	476	
	506	16	477	
	505	17	478	
	504	18	479	
	503	19	480	
	502	20	481	
	501	21	482	
Pindar B. C. 522–443.	500	22	483	Not many years earlier or later than this Jeshua was succeeded by Joiakim as high priest.
	499	23	484	
	498	24	485	
Battle of Lake Regillus.	497	25	486	
	496	26	487	
	495	27	488	
	494	28	489	
Æschylus B. C. 525–456.	493	29	490	
Persian expedition against Greece, under Mardonius.	492	30	491	
Aristides in Athens. Miltiades in Athens.	491	31	492	
The Persians defeated at Marathon.	490	32	493	
	489	33	494	
	488	34	495	
	487	35	496	
Revolt of Eygpt from Persia. Death of Darius Hystaspis. Accession of Xerxes. *a*	486	36	497	
Xerxes conquers Egypt, 1st and 2nd years.	485	1	498	
Xerxes prepares to invade Greece, 2nd to 5th years. Themistocles successful against Aristides.	484	2	499	
	483	3	500	Feast of Ahasuerus (Xerxes) Vashti deposed (Esth. 1).

NOTES.

a B. C. 481. The historical value of the book of Esther consists mainly in the picture it gives of the situation of the Jewish people at that time, and this value remains even if one regards the story as a parable. The narrative fits into the Greek accounts of Xerxes. The really great though vainglorious Xerxes is the same character who is drawn by the Greek historians, though the lines of the drawing are utterly different. The dated events of the book of Esther fit into those given in the Greek accounts. For example, it is interesting to note that while Xerxes was preparing and leading his expedition against Greece—the mightiest expedition till then known in history—he maintained his high and mighty attitude concerning Vashti; but "he remembered Vashti" when he came home disgusted, after the defeats at Thermopylæ and Salamis.

b A. Di. 525. Attempts have been made to identify the Artaxerxes of Ezra and Nehemiah with one of the kings later than Longimanus, but the attempts are not successful.

EXPLANATIONS OF THE DATES.

The deposition of Vashti is dated in the third year of Xerxes (Esth. 1:3). The dates concerning Esther are either expressly stated or given by implication in Esther 2:16, 12, 1-4.

The date of the promotion of Haman is conjectural, but within narrow limits.

The dates for the casting of the lot, the writing of the decree, Mordecai's letters, the time appointed for the slaughter, the days of vengeance, are given in Esther 3:7 3:12; 8:9; 3:7, 13 and 8:12 and 9:1, etc. 9:1, 13, 15, 17, 18 19, 21.

THE TABLES   167

FOREIGN DATED EVENTS.	B. C.	PERSIA. XERXES.	A. DI.	ISRAELITISH DATED EVENTS.
Xerxes preparing to invade Greece. *a*	482	4	501	
	481	5	502	
Persians defeated at Thermopylæ. Defeated at Salamis, September.	480	6	503	Ahasuerus remembers Vashti (Esth. 2). Esther in training 12 months (2:5-15).
Mardonius defeated at Platæa, September.	479	7	504	Esther taken to Ahasuerus, 10th month (Esth. 2:16-23).
Anaxagoras teaching philosophy at Athens B. C. 480-450.	478	8	505	
	477	9	506	
	476	10	507	? Haman promoted (Esth. 3:1-4).
	475	11	508	⎧ Haman's plot and its defeat (Esth. 3-9). Haman casting lots early 1st month. Decree for destruction, 13th day of 1st month.
	474	12	509	⎨ Esther's intervention (Esth. 4-7). Mordecai's letters, 3d mo., 23d day (Esth. 8).
	473	13	510	Appointed time of slaughter, 12th month, 13th day.
	472	14	511	⎩ Days of vengeance, 12th mo., 13th, 14th, 15th days.
	471	15	512	Subsequent events (Esth. 9:20-10:3).
	470	16	513	
	469	17	514	
	468	18	515	
	467	19	516	
Sophocles B. C. 496-406.	466	20	517	Not many years earlier or later than this Joiakim was succeeded by Eliashib as high priest. See "Explanations" on preceding leaf.
Death of Xerxes. Accession of Artaxerxes Longimanus.	465	21	518	
First year of Artaxerxes.	464	1	519	
	463	2	520	
	462	3	521	⎧ Ezra goes to Jerusalem, 7th year *b* of Artaxerxes (Ezra 7-10). Starts 1st day of 1st month; leaves Ahava 12th day; reaches Jerusalem 1st day of 5th month (Ezra 7:7-9, 8:31-33).
	461	4	522	
	460	5	523	⎨ The convocation in the rain, 20th day of 9th month (Ezra 10:9).
	459	6	524	Trying those who had married foreign wives, 1st day of 10th month to 1st day of 1st month (10:16-17).
	458	7	525	⎩

Notes.

For the interval of 58 years between the completion of the temple in B. C. 515 and the going up of Ezra in B. C. 458 we have no direct information concerning the Jews in Palestine. That they had not been in a high degree either faithful or prosperous may be inferred from the state of things as found by Ezra and Nehemiah.

The account in Ezra 3 does not speak of the fortifying of the city; but in the conditions then existing that was an immediate necessity, and we may be sure that it was not neglected. The strongly built temple may have been a part of a scheme of fortification (Ezra 5: 8, 6: 4, 4: 12-16). It is a matter of course that Ezra found the city fortified.

Thirteen years later Nehemiah heard that the walls of the city were full of broken places, and that the gates had been burned. The natural inference for explaining this is that it had resulted from Ezra's interference with the marriages with foreign women. This had led to hostilities, and the party that held with Ezra had been worsted. Later, like attempts were made, but Nehemiah succeeded in foiling them.

Explanations of the Dates.

The blank spaces are here significant. Virtually all the recorded events for the 26 years from the 7th to the 32d of Artaxerxes belong either to the first year of Ezra or the first year of Nehemiah.

Nehemiah received the bad news in the month Chislev of the twentieth year, the ninth month counted vernally, and afterward asked leave of the king in the month Nisan of the twentieth year (Neh. 1: 1, 2: 1). If the numbers are correctly given we have here one of two exceptional uses of language. Either the years are counted autumnally, or else the writer has in mind the Nisan directly following the twentieth year, instead of the Nisan with which that year began.

The building of the wall took 52 days, and was finished the twenty-fifth day of Elul (Neh. 6: 15), the sixth month. Therefore it began about the third day of the fifth month. It agrees with this that the usury incident (Neh. 5) occurred in the season of the new crops.

In the account of the great convocation there are specifications concerning the first day of the seventh month, the second day, the week of the booths (that is, the fifteenth to the twenty-third days, see Lev. 23: 33-36), the twenty-fourth day (Neh. 8: 2, 13, 18 and 9: 1).

It is specified that this first administration of Nehemiah lasted 12 years, and terminated the thirty-second year of Artaxerxes (Neh. 5: 14, 13: 6).

THE TABLES

Foreign Dated Events.	B. C.	Persia. Artax. Lon.	A. Di.	Israelitish Dated Events.
	457	8	526	Trying the cases of those who had married foreign wives completed 1st mo., 1st day (Ezra 10:17).
	456	9	527	
Herodotus B. C. 484-424.	455	10	528	
	454	11	529	
	453	12	530	
	452	13	531	
First decemvirate at Rome.	451	14	532	
	450	15	533	
	449	16	534	
	448	17	535	
	447	18	536	
	446	19	537	
Euripides B. C. 480-406.	445	20	538	Bad news from Jerusalem, month Chislev (Neh. 1.)
Pericles becomes supreme at Athens.	444	21	539	First year's work of Nehemiah (Neh. 2:1-11:2).
The parthenon at Athens built by Phidias B. C. 443-438.	443	22	540	He asks leave of the king, Nisan. Goes to Jerusalem, makes preparation (Neh. 2).
	442	23	541	Wall begun about 3rd day of 5th month.
	441	24	542	Building the wall (Neh. 3-6). The usury outcry (Neh. 5).
Thucydides B. C. 471-403.	440	25	543	Wall completed 25th day of 6th month.
	439	26	544	Great convocation 7th month (Neh. 7-9).
	438	27	545	Subsequent arrangements (Neh. 10 and 11:1-2).
	437	28	546	
	436	29	547	
	435	30	548	
	434	31	549	
	433	32	550	Close of Nehemiah's first administration.

NOTES.

EXPLANATIONS OF THE DATES.

Many date the beginning of Nehemiah's second administration in B. C. 433 or 432. In fact, we have no information as to when it began, but his interval of absence was probably not long.

The situation in the book of Malachi—the remissness of the people in supporting the priests and temple servants, the consequent remissness of the latter in their duties, the foreign marriages, and the strenuous protest against these—is accurately that of the beginning of Nehemiah's second administration.

Eliashib must have been an old man when Nehemiah returned and interfered with his arrangements concerning the temple. It is not probable that he retained the high-priesthood long after that, though very likely his term closed naturally by his death.

Josephus says that Sanballat was "sent into Samaria as satrap by Darius the last king" (*Ant.* XI, vii, 2). In the following sections he speaks as if this Darius were the king with whom the Persian monarchy closed, being overthrown by Alexander the Great. In this he is mistaken, his knowledge of Persian history being hazy, as usual. Nevertheless he may here be following a correct tradition. Sanballat may have been appointed by Darius Nothus, the last king before the "other Artaxerxes" spoken of in the section, namely Artaxerxes Mnemon. Nothing could be more natural than that Darius should favor Sanballat, as his predecessor had favored Nehemiah.

THE TABLES

Foreign Dated Events.	B. C.	Persia. Artax. Lon.	A. Di.	Israelitish Dated Events.
	432	33	551	Not long after Nehemiah's departure, Eliashib, the high priest, gives Tobiah a chamber in the house of God, and things generally go wrong (Neh. 13:4-6, 10 and context).
Peloponnesian war begun, lasting 27 years.	431	34	552	
	430	35	553	At a date not specified Nehemiah comes back as governor, dedicates the wall, renews the provision for the temple servants (Neh. 12:27–13:14).
	429	36	554	
	428	37	555	MALACHI.
Comedies of Aristophanes, B. C. 427-388.	427	38	556	Not many years earlier or later than this Joiada succeeds Eliashib as high priest (Neh. 13:28 and 12:10, 11, 22).
	426	39	557	
	425	40	558	
Death of Artaxerxes. Accession of Darius Nothus.	424	41	559	
First year of Darius. Alcibiades B. C. 450-404.	423	1	560	? Sanballat made satrap in Samaria.
Socrates B. C. 470-399.	422	2	561	
Hippocrates B. C. 460-377.	421	3	562	
	420	4	563	
	419	5	564	
	418	6	565	
	417	7	566	Nehemiah remains governor till he is a very old man (Jos. *Ant.* XI, v, 8), and attends to many matters of enrolment and administration and reform (Neh. 11:3–13:31).
	416	8	567	
Expedition of Nicias to Sicily, B. C. 415-413.	415	9	568	
	414	10	569	
	413	11	570	
Persia intriguing with Sparta and Athens.	412	12	571	
	411	13	572	
	410	14	573	
Second invasion of Sicily by the Carthaginians.	409	15	574	
	408	16	575	

Explanation of the Dates.

"And of the sons of Joiada the high priest there was a son-in-law to Sanballat the Horonite, and I expelled him from beside me" (Neh. 13: 28). This seems to be a condensed account of the incident given in Josephus (*Ant.* XI, vii and viii). Josephus gives the names, and says that Manasseh was the brother of Jaddua, and was excluded in favor of Jaddua.

The statements of Nehemiah seem to imply that the marriage of Manasseh occurred before Joiada was succeeded by Johanan, and that the exclusion was accomplished while Johanan was high priest. For the date of the enrolment the text in Nehemiah gives five points.

First, it followed an earlier enrolment made "in the days of Joiakim" (Neh. 12: 12-21 cf. 26 *a*).

Second, by general description it was "in the days of Eliashib, Joiada, and Johanan and Jaddua" (Neh. 12: 22).

Third, it was "in the days of Nehemiah the governor, and of Ezra the priest, the scribe" (Neh. 12: 26*b*).

Fourth, it was "upon the kingdom of Darius the Persian" (Neh. 12: 22).

Fifth, it was "up to the days of Johanan the son of Eliashib" (Neh. 12: 23).

Noteworthy is the fact that this enrolment, expressly limiting itself by the "days of Johanan," yet includes the name of his successor, Jaddua. A natural explanation of this is found in the inference that Jaddua was enrolled as a part of the proceedings for the exclusion of Manasseh.

According to these data, these events occurred in the lifetime of Nehemiah and his contemporary Sanballat, and some of them before the death of Ezra. Some of them occurred in the reign of Darius, presumably Darius Nothus, the successor of the Artaxerxes of whom the narrative has been speaking. Being "up to the days of Johanan," it cannot have been the later Darius, for he did not reign till many years after the death of this Johanan. Clearly the Samaritan schism and the accession of Johanan occurred in the latter part of the reign of Darius Nothus, probably in the closing decade of the fifth century B. C.

There are confirmations of this. According to the Talmuds Simon, the son of Onias, was the high priest who came out to meet Alexander the Great when he marched upon Jerusalem in B. C. 332 (see the story in Jos. *Ant.* XI, viii, 4-5, though Josephus says that the high priest was Jaddua). Simon was preceded by Onias for 19 years, and he by Jaddua for 20 years, and he by Johanan for 32 years. Now 332 plus 19 plus 20 plus 32 gives us B. C. 403 as the latest possible date for the accession of Johanan, and a few years earlier as the probable date for that accession.

This is confirmed by the passage in 2 Maccabees 1: 23, which speaks of this Jonathan (Johanan) as contemporary with Nehemiah.

Against this is the fact that Josephus, in considerable detail, represents that Jaddua, and not Simon, was high priest in the time of Alexander, and thus dates this group of events about B. C. 330. In this, however, he contradicts his own testimony, as well as that of the other sources of information.

Following Josephus some books of reference date the accession of Johanan about B. C. 371, or later. This makes the four pontificates of Jeshua, Joiakim, Eliashib and Joiada to have extended over more than 167 years, which is incredible; while it is easily credible that they may have extended over the 130 years required by the date given to Johanan in the table.

Simon the son of Onias had been succeeded by Eleazar as high priest before B. C. 285, the date of the scheme for the Alexandrian translation of the Old Testament (Jos. *Ant.* XII, ii and other sources). This proves that Jaddua cannot possibly have been high priest about B. C. 330, for we must here find room for the 40 years of Simon, and the 19 years of Onias who was father to Simon and son to Jaddua.

(*Continued on page 174.*)

THE TABLES

Foreign Dated Events.	B. C.	Persia. Dar. Nothus.	A. Di.	Israelitish Dated Events.
	407	17	576	Not many years earlier or later than this occurred the Samaritan schism, including the following events.
Dionysius tyrant of Syracuse B. C. 405-367.	406	18	577	
Death of Darius Nothus. Accession of Artaxerxes Mnemon.	405	19	578	Manasseh, of the family of Joiada the high priest, married Nicaso, of the family of Sanballat (Neh. 13:28; Jos. *Ant.* XI, vii, 2, and viii).
First year of Artaxerxes Mnemon.	404	1	579	
Thrasybulus restores democracy at Athens.	403	2	580	Joiada, the high priest, was succeeded by Johanan (Neh. 12: 22, 23), otherwise called Jonathan or John (Neh. 12:11; Jos. *Ant.* XI, vii).
Xenophon B. C. 430-357.	402	3	581	
Revolt of Cyrus against Artaxerxes. Cyrus slain at Cunaxa. Retreat of the 10,000 Greeks.	401	4	582	Manasseh, apparently the son of Johanan, was excluded from the high priesthood in favor of his brother Jaddua.
Plato B. C. 429-347.	400	5	583	
Ctesias, the historian. Death of Socrates.	399	6	584	An enrolment was made, "up to the days of Johanan," but including Jaddua his son in the high priestly succession (Neh. 12:10-23).
Isocrates B. C. 436-338.	398	7	585	
	397	8	586	Sanballat made Manasseh priest of the rival temple which he now established at Mount Gerizim, and many of the priests followed the fortunes of this temple (Jos. *Ant.* XI, viii).
	396	9	587	
	395	10	588	
Corinthian war B. C. 394-387.	394	11	589	
	393	12	590	
	392	13	591	
	391	14	592	After these events the completing of the Old Testament, and the death of Nehemiah.
	390	15	593	
	389	16	594	
	388	17	595	
Asian Greek cities submit to Persia. Rome burnt by the Gauls.	387	18	596	Not far from this time Johanan slays his brother Jeshua in the temple, and Bagoses, the general of "another Artaxerxes' army," oppresses the Jews 7 years (Jos. *Ant.* XI, vii).
	386	19	597	
	385	20	598	
	384	21	599	
	383	22	600	

Explanation of the Dates.

(Continued from page 172.)

When Josephus connects with the schism the names of Sanballat and of Jaddua he is correct and thus corroborates the Bible account. Though he omits to speak of the relations of Sanballat with Nehemiah, no one doubts that the Bible is correct in representing that the two were contemporary. Therefore Josephus is mistaken when he assigns to Sanballat a date two or three generations after the death of Nehemiah.

According to Nehemiah the high priesthood of Johanan seems to have begun in the reign of Darius Nothus, and extended on into the reign of Artaxerxes Mnemon.

The sources used by Josephus corroborate this when they represent that John (Jonathan, that is, Johanan) was high priest in the reign of "another Artaxerxes," and that Sanballat had been made satrap by Darius the "last king" before that Artaxerxes (*Ant.* XI, vii); though Josephus himself is badly mixed in his ideas of the Persian kings, and perhaps thought that this Darius was Codomannus. The attempt to identify Bagoses, the general of this other Artaxerxes, with the Egyptian eunuch Bagoas of the time of Artaxerxes Ochus is not successful.

These events connected with the Samaritan schism are the latest mentioned in the connected narrative of the Old Testament, and the latest clearly identifiable events of any character except in predictive passages. No position can be more inconsistent than that of a man who, against Josephus, dates the Samaritan schism about B. C. 400 or earlier, and yet speaks of the mention of Jaddua and of other like items as indicating a date in the Greek period.

THE TABLES

FOREIGN DATED EVENTS.	B. C.	ARTAX. MNEMON.	A. Di.	ISRAELITISH DATED EVENTS.
Olynthian war B. C. 383-379.	382	23	601	
	381	24	602	
	380	25	603	
	379	26	604	
	378	27	605	
	377	28	606	
	376	29	607	
	375	30	608	
	374	31	609	Not many years earlier or later than this the 32 years of the high priest Johanan end, and the 20 years of Jaddua begin.
	373	32	610	
Peace between Athens and Sparta.	372	33	611	
Epaminondas beats the Spartans at Leuctra.	371	34	612	
Phocion B. C. 402-317.	370	35	613	
	369	36	614	
	368	37	615	
Aristotle with Plato at Athens B. C. 367-348.	367	38	616	
	366	39	617	
	365	40	618	
Licinian laws passed at Rome.	364	41	619	
	363	42	620	
Death of Epaminondas at Mantinea.	362	43	621	
	361	44	622	
Aeschines B. C. 389-314.	360	45	623	
Philip, king of Macedonia. Death of Artaxerxes Mnemon. Accession of Ochus.	359	46	624	
First year of Artaxerxes Ochus.	358	1	625	

FOURTH TABLE

FROM THE CLOSE OF OLD TESTAMENT HISTORY

Introduction.

The subject of this volume is Old Testament Chronology. With the times later than the Old Testament it has nothing to do except for their bearings on Old Testament questions. At some points, for example the Maccabæan times, these bearings are important.

There is no attempt to include all the postbiblical Jewish dated events. The records are too full for that. Relatively a few events are included in the table, and preference is given to those that bear on the chronological problems.

The various histories of the times between the close of the Old Testament and the Christian era give dates in terms of the reigns of kings and leaders; but they also make use of various eras, those for example of the olympiads or of the founding of Rome, or of the Roman consulates. As the books of the Maccabees and Josephus give the dates in the terms of the Seleucid era, up to the close of the Maccabæan period, that era, up to that time, is included in the table. From that point the table follows the sources in giving the dates in terms of the years of the Jewish high priests and rulers.

Heretofore in this volume we have dealt almost exclusively with the Jewish and Babylonian vernal year, the year that begins with a new moon in March. Now, however, we come into contact with years of various kinds. The Roman year was vernal, but began differently from the Jewish. The Olympian year began at a varying point early in July. The Seleucid year is said to have begun in September. Other variations may supposably enter into the problem.

These variations have been worked up by scholars with great industry and painstaking. Especial acuteness has been shown in bringing in variations of years in the attempts to solve the numerical problems presented in the book of Daniel. Into matters of this kind the present treatment does not enter. For purposes of ordinary historical chronology, most of these intricacies may safely be neglected.

It is obvious that the sources from which Josephus draws, and Josephus himself, following his sources, use their numerals mainly as the Old Testament writers do.

They have the same habit of treating years as units, rather than as measures of time, and so of counting the difference between two numbers inclusively (see 19 in the Introduction to this volume). For example, Josephus says that Pompey took Jerusalem on the fast day in the third month, B. C. 63, and that Herod took it the same day of the same month in B. C. 37, just 27 years later (see references in the table). He counts the terminal years inclusively, making the difference 27 instead of 26.

They have the same habit of counting a terminal fraction of a year as a whole year, and so sometimes of counting it to both the outgoing and the incoming king. See instances in the table at B. C. 66 and 40. It might be possible to transfer the overlaps there set down to the termination of some other reigns, but they necessarily come in somewhere.

These authors are in the habit of using Jewish vernal years for the ordinary events which they narrate. Josephus himself does this freely, in spite of his giving us the information that the vernal is the sacred year, and that the autumnal year is the proper one for secular events. They use the Jewish vernal year even when they are counting in the Seleucid era. The dates which Josephus gives in olympiads for the sieges of Jerusalem by Pompey and Herod show that the capture in the third month was earlier than July, that is, that he was thinking of a vernal year. The same thing appears when we notice that Herod came out of winter quarters to the siege, and that it lasted five months (*Wars* I, xvii, 8 and xviii, 2; *Ant.* XIV, xv, 14).

The temple was restored the ninth month, Chislev, the 148th year of the Seleucid era (1 Mac. 4:52). Jonathan became high priest the seventh month, at the feast of Tabernacles in the 160th year (1 Mac. 10:21). The death of Simon was in Shebat the eleventh month, the 177th year (1 Mac. 16:14). Other instances are numerous when we interpret them by these.

For some purposes the Jew of those times thought of the year as beginning in March. If he described it in terms of the Greek era, that did not change his idea of the thing itself. What he had in mind was not the year that began in September, but the year that began the preceding March. If he described it by the numerals of an olympiad he may still have meant not the year that began in July, but the one that began the preceding March.

This use of language certainly prevails among these writers. Our table is based on the idea that this was the prevailing usage. They are correct, unless in some particular instances some author has resorted to a different use of terms. If any one thinks that to be the case, he must work out the exceptional instances by themselves.

THE TABLES

Foreign Dated Events.	B.C.	Persia. Art. Mnemon.	Israelitish Dated Events.
	375	30	
	374	31	Not many years earlier or later than this Johanan succeeded by Jaddua, who was high priest 20 years.
	373	32	
	372	33	
	371	34	
	370	35	
	369	36	
	368	37	
	367	38	
	366	39	
	365	40	
	364	41	
	363	42	
	362	43	
	361	44	
	360	45	
Artaxerxes Mnemon succeeded by Ochus.	359	46	
First year of Artaxerxes Ochus.	358	1	
	357	2	
Birth of Alexander the Great.	356	3	
	355	4	
	354	5	Not many years earlier or later than this, Jaddua succeeded by Onias I, who was high priest 19 years.
	353	6	
Orations of Demosthenes B. C. 352–330.	352	7	
	351	8	

Foreign Dated Events.	B. C.	Persia. Art. Ochus.	Alexander the Great.	Israelitish Dated Events.
Aristotle B. C. 384–322.	350	9		*Note.*—The Talmuds say that Simon I was high priest in the time of Alexander, and held the office 40 years, that is, about B. C. 335–295. Josephus (*Ant.* XII, ii, 5 and iv, 1) agrees with the other traditions in saying that this Simon (not Simon II, son of Onias II) is the distinguished Simon the Just.
Olynthian war B. C. 349–347.	349	10		
	348	11		
	347	12		
Philip captures Phocis, and is admitted to Amphyctionic council.	346	13		
	345	14		The Men of the Great Synagogue are mentioned in the traditions as a succession of men (not as an official body) including Daniel and his associates and inferentially Ezekiel, together with all the later prophets and great men of the Old Testament, and terminating with Simon the Just, Ezra, however, being the great representative name. The traditions attribute the completing of the Old Testament to the prophets who were of this succession.
	344	15		
	343	16		
Philip invades Thrace.	342	17		
	341	18		
	340	19		
	339	20		Not many years earlier or later than this, Onias I succeeded by Simon I, who was high priest 40 years.
Battle of Cheronea. Greece subjugated to Philip. Death of Artax. Ochus.	338	21		
Rome conquers Latium B C. 337–335. Dissensions in Persia. noted in Canon as the two years of Arogus.	337	1		
Alexander succeeds Philip.	336	2		
First year of Darius Codomannus.	335	1		
Alexander defeats the Persians on the Granicus, May 22d.	334	2		
Alexander defeats Darius at Issus, October.	333	3		
Alexander marches through Palestine, besieges Tyre, founds Alexandria in Egypt.	332	4		Alexander favors both the Jews and the Samaritans, both in Palestine and as citizens of Alexandria.
First year of Alexander as successor of Darius.	331		1	
	330		2	
	329		3	
	328		4	
Alexander in India, B. C. 327–325.	327		5	
	326		6	

THE TABLES

Foreign Dated Events.	B. C.	Alexander the Great.	Seleucid Era.	Israelitish Dated Events.
	325	7		
	324	8		
Death of Alexander. First year of Ptolemy Lagus in Egypt as counted in the Canon, though in fact the history was more complicated than this would suggest. Lagus is also called Soter.	323	1		
	322	2		
The Romans surrender to the Samnites.	321	3		
	320	4		
	319	5		
	318	6		Ptolemy, early in his reign, subjugated Palestine, and treated the Jews with mingled cruelty and favor.
	317	7		
Berosus the Babylonian historian contemporary with Alexander and Ptolemy Lagus.	316	8		
	315	9		
	314	10		
	313	11		
First year of Seleucus Nicator as king in Syria. Seleucus and Ptolemy defeat Demetrius at Gaza.	312	12	1	"Year of the kingdom of the Greeks" (1 Mac. 1:10, etc.).
	311	13	2	This erà is important in biblical chronology because in it the books of Maccabees and Josephus date the events of the Maccabæan times.
Epicurus B. C. 342-270.	310	14	3	
	309	15	4	Properly, it is said, the Seleucid year begins in the autumn. But the years intended by the Jewish writers are, in some cases, at least, vernal years, the years beginning in the preceding March (e. g. 1 Mac. 4:52, 10:21, 16:14). The table is made on the basis of this usage. In a few instances the difference between the autumnal and the vernal years may require a correction in a date, but that is doubtful.
	308	16	5	
	307	17	6	
	306	18	7	
	305	19	8	
	304	20	9	
	303	21	10	
	302	22	11	
Battle of Ipsus. Final division of Alexander's dominions.	301	23	12	

Foreign Dated Events.	B. C.	Ptolemy Lagus.	Seleucid Era.	Israelitish Dated Events.
Antioch in Syria founded.	300	24	13	Religious controversies in Egypt between Jews and Samaritans. Partial translations of Old Testament into Greek (Jos. *Ant.* XII, i and ii).
	299	25	14	
	298	26	15	
	297	27	16	
	296	28	17	
? Beginnings of Alexandrian Library.	295	29	18	? Eleazar succeeds Simon I as high priest.
Demetrius Phalereus, after a famous career at Athens, was for many years a favorite of Ptolemy Lagus, and active in founding the Library.	294	30	19	? Ecclesiasticus written. It was translated into Greek by the grandson of the author about "the 38th year upon Euergetes," that is, either B. C. 234 or B. C. 133 (see table). It celebrates (Ecclus. 50: 1-21) Simon the son of Onias, who died about B. C. 295 or 199 (see table). The earlier dates are the true ones, though many prefer the later.
	293	31	20	
	292	32	21	
	291	33	22	
	290	34	23	
	289	35	24	
	288	36	25	
	287	37	26	
	286	38	27	
Ptolemy Philadelphus associated with Lagus on the throne.	285	39 / 1	28	The Septuagint begun, in a plan of Demetrius Phalereus for placing the Old Testament books in the Alexandrian Library (Jos. *Ant.* XII, ii).
	284	40 / 2	29	
Death of Lagus. Exit Demetrius Phalereus.	283	41 / 3	30	
	282	4	31	Josephus says that in these times the Jews were in favor not only in Alexandria but in Antioch, and in the many other Greek cities that were founded in the Orient (*Ant.* XII, iii).
	281	5	32	
Death of Seleucus Nicator. Accession of Antiochus Soter. Invasion of Italy by Pyrrhus.	280	6	33	
The Gauls invade Greece.	279	7	34	
	278	8	35	
	277	9	36	
	276	10	37	

THE TABLES

Foreign Dated Events.	B. C.	Ptolemy Philadel.	Seleucid Era.	Israelitish Dated Events.
	275	11	38	
Pyrrhus driven from Italy.	274	12	39	
Alexandria busy for generations with the Greek classics.	273	13	40	
	272	14	41	
First year of Ptolemy Euergetes I as coregnant with Philadelphus (Mahaffy *Ptol. Dyn.* p. 99).	271	15	42	
? Theocritus in Alexandria.	270	16	43	
	269	17	44	
	268	18	45	
	267	19	46	
	266	20	47	
Rome supreme over Italy.	265	21	48	
The Punic wars begin. Close of the Parian Chronicle.	264	22	49	
	263	23	50	
	262	24	51	
Death of Antiochus Soter. Accession of Antiochus Theos.	261	25	52	
	260	26	53	? Eleazar succeeded by Manasseh as high priest.
The coregnancy of Euergetes with Philadelphus ceases (see at B. C. 271).	259	27	54	Great favors to the Jews in these years from Antiochus Theos (Jos. *Ant.* XII, iii, 3).
	258	28	55	
Archimedes B. C. 287–212.	257	29	56	
	256	30	57	
	255	31	58	
	254	32	59	
	253	33	60	
	252	34	61	
	251	35	62	

THE TABLES

Foreign Dated Events.	B. C.	Ptolemy Philadel.	Seleucid Era.	Israelitish Dated Events.
Arsaces, king in Parthia, circa. About this time Manetho in Egypt.	250	36	63	Some scholars hold that the books of Chronicles were not written till about this date.
	249	37	64	
	248	38	65	
Death of Philadelphus. Accession of Euergetes I as sole king.	247	39	66	
Ptolemy captures Antioch (Mahaffy *Ptol. Dyn.* p. 105ff.). Death of Antiochus Theos and accession of Seleucus Callinicus.	246	1	67	
	245	2	68	
	244	3	69	
	243	4	70	
	242	5	71	
End of first Punic war.	241	6	72	
Plays of Livius Andronicus at Rome.	240	7	73	
	239	8	74	
The Canopus inscription (Mahaffy *Ptol. Dyn.* p. 111ff.).	238	9	75	
	237	10	76	
	236	11	77	
The gate of Janus shut.	235	12	78	
	234	13	79	38th year of Euergetes, counting from the 15th year of Philadelphus, which see. ? Translation of Ecclesiasticus (see at B. C. 300-276).
	233	14	80	
	232	15	81	? Manasseh succeeded by Onias II as high priest.
	231	16	82	
	230	17	83	About this date begins the career of more than 22 years of Joseph the son of Tobias (Jos. *Ant.* XII, iv).
	229	18	84	
	228	19	85	
	227	20	86	
Death of Seleucus Callinicus. Accession of Seleucus Keraunos.	226	21	87	

THE TABLES

Foreign Dated Events.	B. C.	Ptolemy Euergetes I.	Seleucid Era.	Israelitish Dated Events.
	225	22	88	
	224	23	89	
Death of Seleucus Keraunos. Accession of Antiochus the great.	223	24	90	
Death of Ptolemy Euergetes I. Accession of Ptolemy Philopator.	222	25	91	
	221	1	92	
	220	2	93	? Birth of Hyrcanus, son of Joseph (Jos. *Ant.* XII, iv).
	219	3	94	? Onias II succeeded as high priest by Simon II, sometimes wrongly identified with Simon the Just, and with the Simon of Ecclesiasticus 50.
	218	4	95	
In these years wars between Ptolemy and Antiochus, in which Palestine was ravaged.	217	5	96	
	216	6	97	*Note.*—The books of reference say that the first Cleopatra of Egypt was the wife whom Ptolemy Epiphanes married after B.C. 198. This contradicts Josephus. He represents Hyrcanus as dealing with a Cleopatra, wife of a Ptolemy, before the death of the high priest Simon, and Joseph as doing the same many years earlier.
	215	7	98	
	214	8	99	
	213	9	100	
	212	10	101	
First Macedonian war with Rome B. C. 211–205.	211	11	102	
Attalus, king of Pergamos B. C. 241–197.	210	12	103	
	209	13	104	
	208	14	105	
	207	15	106	? Hyrcanus at court of Ptolemy at 13 years of age (*Ant.* XII, iv, 6).
	206	16	107	
Death of Ptolemy Philopator. Accession of Ptolemy Epiphanes at 5 years of age.	205	17	108	
	204	1	109	
In the earlier part of his reign Ptolemy successful against Antiochus.	203	2	110	
	202	3	111	
End of second Punic war.	201	4	112	

Foreign Dated Events.	B. C.	Ptolemy Epiphanes.	Seleucid Era.	Israelitish Dated Events.
Second Macedonian war, B. C. 200–197.	200	5	113	? Death of Joseph. His sons quarrel. Simon takes sides against Hyrcanus.
	199	6	114	? Simon II succeeded by Onias III.
Antiochus the great defeats Ptolemy Epiphanes in a decisive battle at Banias, and at some later date marries his daughter Cleopatra to him, giving him an interest in Palestine as dowry.	198	7	115	The Jews eagerly accept Antiochus, and are received by him with great favor.
	197	8	116	The writing of Ecclesiasticus is by some dated about this time. See at B. C. 300–276.
	196	9	117	
Cato, the elder, consul.	195	10	118	
	194	11	119	
	193	12	120	
War between the Romans and Antiochus the great.	192	13	121	
	191	14	122	
	190	15	123	
	189	16	124	
	188	17	125	
Death of Antiochus. Accession of Seleucus Philopator.	187	18	126	
	186	19	127	
	185	20	128	
	184	21	129	
	183	22	130	
	182	23	131	
Death of Ptolemy Epiphanes. Accession of Ptolemy Philometer.	181	24	132	Hyrcanus reigns beyond the Jordan the last seven years of Seleucus Philopator (Jos. *Ant.* XII, iv, 11).
	180	1	133	
	179	2	134	
	178	3	135	In the reign of Seleucus the incident of Onias and Heliodorus (2 Mac. 3-4).
	177	4	136	Notice of a translation of Esther —"fourth year of the reign of Ptolemy and Cleopatra" (Apocryphal Esther 11 : 1).
	176	5	137	

Foreign Dated Events.	B.C.	Ptolemy Philometer.	Seleucid Era.	Israelitish Dated Events.
Seleucus Philopator succeeded by Antiochus Epiphanes. [According to 1 Maccabees 1 : 10 "the 137th year of the Kingdom of the Greeks" B. C. 176.]	175	6	138	
	174	7	139	Onias III deposed in favor of Jason (Jesus). Antiochus splendidly entertained in Jerusalem.
	173	8	140	
Third Macedonian war B. C. 172–168.	172	9	141	Jason superseded by Menelaus (Onias) "after 3 years." See at B. C. 163. Onias III murdered (2 Mac. 4 : 23ff.).
	171	10	142	
First year of Ptolemy Euergetes II (Physkon) as coregnant with Philometer.	170	11	143	Antiochus captures Jerusalem. Horrible details. "143d year" (1 Mac. 1 : 20).
	169	12	144	
	168	13	145	Horrors "after 2 full years." Abomination on the altar. "15th day of Chislev, 145th year" (1 Mac. 1 : 54).
	167	14	146	Judas Maccabæus leader 146th year (1 Mac. 2 : 70).
First comedy of Terence at Rome.	166	15	147	
	165	16	148	Temple restored 25th day of 9th month, Chislev, 148th year (1 Mac. 4 : 52).
Death of Antiochus Epiphanes. Accession of Antiochus Eupator.	164	17	149	Ant. Epiph. died 149th year (1 Mac. 6 : 16). After B. C. 164 letter to Aristobulus (2 Mac. 1 : 18 and 14).
	163	18	150	Judas besieges citadel 150th year (1 Mac. 6 : 20). Menelaus slain, high priest 10 years (Jos. XII, ix, 7). Alcimus (Jacimus) high priest.
Death of Antiochus Eupator. Accession of Demetrius Soter.	162	19	151	Judas defeats Demetrius 13th day of Adar, 151st year (1 Mac. 7 : 1, 49 ; 2 Mac. 14 : 4). Makes treaty with Rome (1 Mac. 8).
	161	20	152	Judas slain 1st month of 152d year. Jonathan succeeds (1 Mac. 9 : 3).
	160	21	153	Alcimus dies 153d year, 2d month (1 Mac. 9 : 54–56). 7 years without a high priest (Jos. Ant. XX, x, 1).
	159	22	154	
	158	23	155	Rest 2 years (1 Mac. 9 : 57).
	157	24	156	After Alcimus became high priest, B. C. 163, and before the death of Ptolemy Philometer, B. C. 146, Onias, son of high priest Onias III, built a Jewish temple at Leontopolis in Egypt (Jos. Ant. XII, v, 1 and ix, 7 ; XIII, iii).
	156	25	157	
	155	26	158	
	154	27	159	
	153	28	160	Demetrius and Alexander Epiphanes seek alliance with Jonathan, 160th year. Jonathan becomes high priest at feast of Tabernacles 7th month of 160th year (1 Mac. 10 : 21).
Alexander Bala (Epiphanes) succeeds Demetrius Soter. Marriage of Alexander with Cleopatra of Egypt 162d year (1 Mac. 10 : 57).	152	29	161	
	151	30	162	

THE TABLES

FOREIGN DATED EVENTS.	B. C.	PTOLEMY PHILOMETER.	SELEUCID ERA.	ISRAELITISH DATED EVENTS.
	150	31	163	Josephus says that about B. C. 150, in the high priesthood of Jonathan, the three Jewish sects, the Pharisees, the Sadducees and the Essenes, were in existence (*Ant.* XIII, v, 9).
Invasion by Demetrius Nicator, 165th year (1 Mac. 10:67). Ptolemy Philometer takes Cleopatra from Alexander Bala, and gives her to Demetrius.	149	32	164	
	148	33	165	Jonathan takes part with Demetrius.
Ptolemy and Demetrius defeat Alexander, 167th year (1 Mac. 11:19). Ptolemy becomes king in Antioch, but dies soon after. Demetrius king in Antioch. Ptolemy Euergetes II sole king in Egypt. Carthage destroyed.	147	34	166	
	146	35	167	? Jonathan renews treaties with Rome and Sparta (1 Mac. 12).
	145	1	168	Jonathan was honored by Demetrius, and afterward treated treacherously by both him and Tryphon.
Tryphon fighting against Demetrius.	144	2	169	
	143	3	170	? Death of Jonathan. First year of Simon, 170th year (1 Mac. 13:41). Judæa independent.
	142	4	171	Simon captures the citadel, 171st year, 2d month, 23d day (1 Mac. 13:51).
Demetrius Nicator captured by Arsaces, 172d year (1 Mac. 14:1).	141	5	172	Third year of Simon his authority made perpetual, 172d year, 18th of Elul (1 Mac. 14:27ff).
	140	6	173	
Antiochus Sidetes, son of Demetrius, attempts to recover power.	139	7	174	Antiochus wars against Tryphon, 174th year (1 Mac. 15:10).
	138	8	175	The Romans recognize the Jews as allies.
	137	9	176	Simon high priest 8 years (Jos. *Ant.* XIII, vii, 4 and XX, x).
	136	10	177	Death of Simon, 177th year, 11th month, Shebat (1 Mac. 16:14). John Hyrcanus succeeds him.
	135	11	1	First year of Hyrcanus. War against him by Antiochus Sidetes (Jos. *Ant.* XIII, viii).
	134	12	2	Treaty with Antiochus soon after feast of Tabernacles.
Laws of Gracchus at Rome.	133	13	3	38th year of Euergetes II (see at B. C. 170). Translation of Ecclesiasticus? See at B. C. 300–276.
	132	14	4	
	131	15	5	*Note.*—From B. C. 135 the Jewish sources cease to give the dates in terms of the Greek era. The years in the table are those of the rule of John Hyrcanus. The reigns in Egypt no longer important in Jewish dates.
	130	16	6	
Antiochus defeated by Arsaces.	129	17	7	
Demetrius Nicator, second reign. Succeeded by Alexander Zebina.	128	18	8	Hyrcanus conquers and circumcises the Idumæans.
	127	19	9	Renews friendship with the Romans.
Alexander succeeded by Antiochus Gryphus.	126	20	10	

THE TABLES

Foreign Dated Events.	B. C.	John Hyrcanus.	Israelitish Dated Events.
First year of Antiochus Gryphus.	125	11	John Hyrcanus high priest and leader from B. C. 135.
	124	12	
	123	13	
	122	14	
	121	15	? Hyrcanus destroys Samaria (Jos. *Ant.* XIII, x).
	120	16	
Marius B. C. 155-86.	119	17	
	118	18	
Death of Ptolemy Euergetes II. Succeeded jointly by his wife Cleopatra and their son Lathyrus, otherwise known as Soter and Philometer.	117	19	Josephus says that Chelkias and Ananias, sons of Onias (see at B. C. 157) were generals and trusted counselors of Cleopatra (*Ant.* XIII, x).
	116	20	
	115	21	
	114	22	At some date Hyrcanus is opposed by the Pharisees, and becomes a Sadducee (*Ant.* XIII, x, 5-7).
Cimbri and Teutones invade Gaul.	113	23	*Note.*—John Hyrcanus 30 years, 31 years, 33 entire years (Jos. *Ant.* XX, x; XIII, x, 7; *Wars* I, ii, 8). As the table shows, the larger number is needed to fill out the interval between the two fixed dates: the first year of Hyrcanus, B. C. 135, and the taking of Jerusalem by Pompey, B. C. 63.
	112	24	
Jugurthine war B. C. 111-106.	111	25	
	110	26	
Roman victories begin over Cimbri and Teutones.	109	27	
	108	28	Josephus' long number for the Asamoneans, 126 or 125 (*Ant.* XIV, xvi, 4 and XVII, vi, 3), appears to have been obtained by adding the reigns from Jonathan, the first Asamonean high priest, and neglecting overlaps. Jonathan 18 years plus Simon 8 plus John Hyrcanus 33 plus Judas Aristobulus 1 plus Alexander Janneas 27 plus Hyrcanus 9 plus Aristobulus 3 plus Hyrcanus 24 plus Antigonus 3 equal 126.
Expelled from Egypt by Cleopatra, in favor of Ptolemy Alexander, Ptolemy Lathyrus still reigns in Cyprus.	107	29	
	106	30	
Sulla B. C. 138-78.	105	31	
	104	32	
	103	33	
	102	1	Judas Aristobulus high priest and king.
End of Cimbrian-Teutonic war.	101	1	Alexander Janneas high priest and king (Jos. *Ant.* XIII, xii, 1).

Foreign Dated Events.	B. C.	Alexander Janneas.	Israelitish Dated Events.
Birth of Julius Caesar.	100	2	Alexander Janneas, third son of John Hyrcanus, high priest and king B. C. 101–75 (Jos. *Ant.* XIII, xii; *Wars* I, iv).
	99	3	
	98	4	
Death of Antiochus Gryphus. Accession of Seleucus Gryphus.	97	5	? Invasion by Ptolemy Lathyrus from Cyprus, followed by alliance of Jews with Cleopatra.
	96	6	
	95	7	
	94	8	
	93	9	
	92	10	
	91	11	
Social war in Italy begins.	90	12	
Death of Cleopatra. Return of Ptolemy Lathyrus to Egypt.	89	13	
Wars of Marius and Sulla begin.	88	14	The reign of Janneas was characterized by wars, both civil and foreign.
	87	15	
	86	16	
	85	17	
	84	18	
	83	19	
	82	20	
Death of Ptolemy Lathyrus.	81	21	Alexander was at variance with the Pharisees, but at his death advised Alexandra to be friends with them.
Accession of Ptolemy Auletes.	80	22	
	79	23	
	78	24	
	77	25	
	76	26	

THE TABLES

FOREIGN DATED EVENTS.	B. C.	ALEXANDER JANNEÆS.	ISRAELITISH DATED EVENTS.
	75	27	Janneas 27 years (*Ant.* XX, x; *Wars* I, iv, 8).
	74	1	Alexandra queen, Hyrcanus high priest, the Pharisees sovereign (*Wars* I, v; *Ant.* XIII, xvi).
Spartacus in Italy.	73	2	
	72	3	Josephus (*Ant.* XIV, i, 2) wrongly dates the accession of Hyrcanus the 3d year of the 177th olympiad, Metellus consul, that is, between April and July B. C. 69.
Spartacus defeated by Crassus.	71	4	
Pompey and Crassus consuls. Cicero B. C. 106–43.	70	5	
Quintus Metellus Creticus consul.	69	6	
Cato the younger B. C. 95–46.	68	7	Alexandra and Hyrcanus 9 years (*Wars* I, v, 4; *Ant.* XIII, xvi, 6 and XX, x). Then Aristobulus high priest and king for 3 years and a fraction (*Ant.* XIV, vi, 1 and XX, x). Here count the overlap of one year.
	67	8	
Pompey ends the Parthian war.	66	9/1	
Lucretius B. C. 96–55.	65	2	Antipater, father of Herod, becomes manager for Hyrcanus.
Pompey makes Syria a province of Rome.	64	3	
Cicero, consul, suppresses Cataline's rebellion.	63	1	Hyrcanus restored by Pompey (*Ant.* XX, x), who took Jerusalem the 3d month of the vernal year, when Cicero was consul, the 179th olympiad (*Ant.* XIV, iv, 3 and xvi, 4), that is, before July B. C. 63.
	62	2	
	61	3	
First triumvirate: Pompey, Caesar, Crassus.	60	4	
	59	5	In these years Hyrcanus is often called king, but he was forbidden the insignia of royalty, and lacked its authority.
Gallic war begins.	58	6	
	57	7	
	56	8	
Caesar invades Britain B. C. 55–54.	55	9	
	54	10	
Crassus defeated and slain by the Parthians.	53	11	Going against the Parthians, Crassus visited Judæa, robbed the temple, etc.
Sallust B. C. 86–34.	52	12	
Gaul completely subjugated.	51	13	

Foreign Dated Events.	B.C.	Hyrcanus, High Priest.	Israelitish Dated Events.
	50	14	
Caesar enters Rome as master.	49	15	
Battle of Pharsalia. Later, death of Pompey.	48	16	Caesar makes Antipater governor, and confirms Hyrcanus as high priest (*Ant.* XIV, viii).
Caesar in Egypt, at war.	47	17	Antipater sets Herod over Galilee. Trial of Herod. Sameas and Pollio (*Ant.* XIV, ix, 4; cf. XV, i, 1 and x, 4).
	46	18	
Year 1 of Julian Era. Year 4669 of Julian Period.	45	19	
Death of Caesar, Mar. 15.	44	20	
Second triumvirate: Octavius, Antony, Lepidus.	43	21	Death of Antipater. Cassius makes Herod governor of all Syria (Jos. *Wars* I, xi and xii).
Battle of Philippi. Death of Cassius.	42	22	The Parthians carry off Hyrcanus and make Antigonus high priest and leader. Herod flees to Rome.
Cleopatra meets Antony at Tarsus.	41	23	
Vergil B. C. 70–19.	40	24 / 1	Herod made king by Roman senate at Antony's wish, 184th olympiad, Pollio consul, B. C. 40 before July (Jos. *Ant.* XIV, xiv, 5).
	39	2	
	38	3	
	37	1	Herod and Sossius capture Jerusalem 185th olympiad, Marcus Agrippa consul, the 3d month of the vernal year, May or June of B. C. 37 (Jos. *Ant.* XIV, xvi, 4). Antigonus was soon after put to death by Antony. In dating events by the reign of Herod, Josephus oftenest counts B. C. 37, not B. C. 40, as Herod's first year.
Exit Lepidus.	36	2	
	35	3	
	34	4	
	33	5	
War between Antony and Octavius.	32	6	The 7th year of Herod, 187th olympiad (Jos. *Ant.* XV, v; *Wars* I, xix). After Actium, Herod obtained favor from Octavius, having slain Hyrcanus (*Wars* I, xx; *Ant.* XV, vi).
Antony overthrown at Actium, Sept. 2d. Octavius sole ruler of Roman empire.	31	7	
Deaths of Antony and Cleopatra.	30	8	
Livy B. C. 59 to A. D. 17. The gate of Janus shut.	29	9	Hillel president of Sanhedrin B. C. 30 to A. D. 9. Shammai colleague of Hillel.
	28	10	*Note.*—Josephus expressly says that Herod reigned 37 years from his being made king by the Roman senate, and 34 years from his succeeding Antigonus (*Ant.* XVII, viii, 1; *Wars* I, xxxiii, 8).
	27	11	
	26	12	

Foreign Dated Events.	B. C.	Herod.	Israelitish Dated Events.
The gate of Janus shut.	25	13	13th of Herod (*Ant.* XV, ix, 1; cf. XV, viii). He establishes quinquennial games, and fortifies Samaria.
	24	14	
	23	15	? Herod makes Simon Boethus high priest, and marries his daughter (*Ant.* XV, ix). Herod begins rebuilding temple, 15th year (*Wars* I, xxi, 1), or 18th (*Ant.* XV, xi).
	22	16
	21	17	He begins to build Caesarea B. C. 22(?), either the 12th or the 10th year (*Ant.* XV, ix, 6 or XVI, v, 1) before its completion in his 28th year.
	20	18
? Philo of Alexandria born.		
	19	19	
	18	20	
Agrippa governor of Syria.	17	21	
	16	22	
Victories of Drusus over the Rhaeti.	15	23	
	14	24	Temple completed 9½ years (Jos. *Ant.* XV, xi, 5 and 6).
Tiberius consul.	13	25	
Death of Agrippa. Drusus invades Germany.	12	26	
Campaigns of Tiberius B. C. 11-9. Tiberius marries the widow of Agrippa.	11	27	
Ovid B. C. 43 to A. D. 18.	10	28	Celebration of the completing of Caesarea. Quinquennial games. 28th year of Herod, in 192d olympiad (Jos. *Ant.* XVI, v, 1; *Wars* I, xxi, 8).
Death of Drusus, brother of Tiberius.	9	29
Tiberius military "imperator" and consul.	8	30
	7	31	
Tiberius tribune, and thus associated with Augustus.	6	32	
	5	33	Birth of Jesus.
	4	34	Death of Herod a few weeks after the eclipse of the moon, March 13, B. C. 4. (*Ant.* XVII, vi, 4 and viii, 1; *Wars* I, xxxiii, 8). Archelaus succeeds.
	3	1
	2	2
	1	3

APPENDIX

This volume has been an unusually long time in going through the press, and some interesting data have become available since the copy for it was written. See, for example, the "Chronicles Concerning Early Babylonian Kings," by Dr. King of the British Museum, or the work done by Professors Hilprecht and Clay, in volumes XX, XIV, XV, of the "Babylonian Expedition" of the University of Pennsylvania. Certain items from these sources have been widely circulated in an article by Professor R. W. Rogers, published August 22, 1907, in the Christian Advocate. It happens that some of these new data gratifyingly confirm some of the positions which I have taken in this volume.

On page 25 I have expressed my acceptance of Professor Hommel's view, published several years since, to the effect that the so-called second dynasty in Babylon, extending over 368 years, was contemporary with other dynasties, so that, for the times before the Babylonian Kassite dynasty, we must subtract this 368 years from the long numbers given by the Assyrian chronologers. When I wrote the section, this view was a mere opinion, held by a small minority. At the present time its correctness has been proved, and it takes its place among ascertained facts. And with its acceptance all doubt vanishes as to the identification of Hammurabi with the Amraphel of Genesis.

On the basis of these data Professor Hilprecht now places the long reign of Hammurabi between B. C. 2,000 and B. C. 1830, and most of the dates which other scholars have proposed can be reduced within those limits.

The settling of the question concerning the Babylonian second dynasty throws light on the methods of the Assyrian chronologers and their Babylonian successors. The documents prove that they did not insert that 368 years by reason of any lack of means of information. If for the glory of Sennacherib and Asshurbanipal and Nabonidus they could add that dynasty to their sum of chronological time, they may also, from similar motives, have omitted a discreditable block of fifty-one years from the time following Ramman-nirari III. This is a slight but appreciable confirmation of the view I have presented on page 19.

On pages 20 ff. I have presented arguments against the theory of Egyptian chronology which dates the accession of Thutmose III in B. C. 1501, and therefore that of Amenôphis IV, the contemporary of Burna-buriash of Babylon, about B. C. 1375. My contention is confirmed by the dated documents published by Professor Clay. These give the following minimum numbers for the years of certain Babylonian kings: Burna-buriash, 25; Kuri-galzu, 23; Nazi-maruttash, 24; Kadashman-turgu, 16; Kadashman-bel II, 6; Kudur-bel, 9. These kings, and others not here named, reigned in the interval between Burna-buriash and Shagashalti-shuriash, who reigned about 800 years before Nabonidus (p. 24). Counting from accession to accession, this gives about B. C. 1355 for Shagashalti-shuriash, and about B. C. 1458 as a minimum for Burna-buriash. If we suppose that these kings reigned on an average three or four years each after the latest dated contract, made in his reign, which modern discoverers have happened to find and read, that will place the accession of Burna-buriash well back toward B. C. 1500 Assyrian; that is, about B. C. 1550 in my tables. Add the omitted reigns, and the date becomes much earlier.

The greatest difficulty in the way of the view which I have presented is the fact that at certain points the Assyrian kings of whom we have knowledge are not numerous enough to fill out the time called for by the chronological numbers (see pages 18, 24 ff., and the tables). For example, my table dates Asshur-uballit about B. C. 1650 (B. C. 1600 Assyrian), and Tukulti-ninip about B. C. 1340 (B. C. 1290 Assyrian), with only six known Assyrian kings to cover the interval (pp. 25, 26). There is a similar blank about B. C. 1120-1000 (B. C. 1070-950 Assyrian), following the reign of Asshur-bel-kala, and another seeming gap, of fifty-one years, between the reign of Ramman-nirari III and B. C. 773 (pp. 18 ff., 108 ff., 136 ff).

Some contributions have been made toward the filling of these gaps, and therefore toward the accrediting of my position. Professor King's discovery of a Tiglathpilezer hitherto unknown is a contribution of this sort. Indirectly bearing in the same direction is the fact that the recent discoveries supply the materials for filling certain gaps in the chronology before the time of Abraham. It is highly probable that processes of this kind will continue. When we recover the knowledge of a few more Assyrian and Babylonian kings, that may positively settle the chronology.

These things confirm me in my judgment as to a certain principle that has governed my treatment alike of the biblical and of the Assyrio-Babylonian numbers. That principle is, *to use the numbers as they stand, except when there is evidence by which to correct them, leaving open the question as to how they are to be reconciled.* Most treatments of the subject adopt the different principle of making conjectural corrections at various points. It is easier to form the best judgment you can on the basis of the evidence now at hand, than it is to suspend judgment and wait for sufficient evidence. I do not find fault with those who take this course. All sorts of hypotheses should be tried in our attempts to reach the truth. But it seems to me that there are especial advantages in a treatment which avoids merely conjectural corrections, and I have tried to present such a treatment.

My tables follow Nabonidus in placing Shagashalti-buriash (or -shuriash) about B. C. 1400 (B. C. 1350 Assyrian), and they follow the Babylonian lists of kings in giving the first year of a king of the same or similar name as B. C. 1297 (B. C. 1246 Assyrian). Are these two different kings? or two mentions of the same king? Many scholars take it for granted that they are the same; but this is one of the questions that must wait for evidence.

TOPICAL INDEX

AARON, 63.
Abdon, 105.
Abijam, 127.
Abimelech of Gerar, 37, 39, 44.
Abimelech, captain of Israel, 97.
Abraham, 37 ff.
Abraham's sons, 38, 42.
Absalom, 80, 81, 119.
Adonijah, 83, 120.
Adu-me-ur, 108.
Aeschines, 175.
Aeschylus, 165.
Aesop, 159.
Africanus, Julius, 8.
Agu-kak-rimi, 108.
Ahab, 131.
Ahaziah of Israel, 133.
Ahaziah of Judah, 131 ff.
Ahasuerus, 165.
Ahaz, 145.
Ahijah, 126.
Alcibiades, 171.
Alcimus, 189.
Alexander Bala, 189.
Alexander the Great, 181.
Alexander Jannaes, 191.
Alexandra, 192, 193.
Alexandria founded, 182.
Alexandrian library, 184.
Amalek and Saul, 114, 115.
Amarna letters, 57, 59.
Amaziah, 137.
Amenhotep II, 53.
Amenhotep III, 57.
Amenhotep IV, 20, 59, 60.
A. Mig., 36.
Ammon, 39, 41.
Ammonite oppression, 102, 103.
Amon, 153.
Amos, 141.
Amram, 59, 69.
Amraphel (see Hammurabi).
Anabasis, the, 173.
Anacreon, 163.
Anarchy eighteen years, 87, 102.
Anaxagoras, 167.
Anno Discidii (A.Di.), 126 ff.
Antioch and the Jews, 184.
Antiochus Epiphanes, 189.
Antiochus Eupator, 189.
Antiochus the Great, 187.
Antiochus Grypus, 190.
Antiochus Sidetes, 190.
Antiochus Soter, 189.
Antiochus Theos, 185.
Antipater, 193.
Antony, 194.
Archelaus, 195.
Archimedes, 185.
Archonship at Athens, 149.
Aristides, 165.
Aristobulus, 193.
Aristobulus, Judas, 191.
Aristophanes, 171.
Aristotle, 175, 182.

Ark brought to Jerusalem, 81, 117.
Artaxerxes Longimanus, 167.
Artaxerxes Mnemon, 173.
Artaxerxes Ochus, 175, 181.
Asa, 126 ff.
Asamoneans 126 years, 191.
Asshurbanipal, 151.
Asshur-bel-kala, 109 ff.
Asshur-daan I, 103.
Asshur-daan II, 127.
Asshur-daan III, 136.
Asshur-nadin-shuma, 149.
Asshur-natsir-pal, 95, 129 ff.
Asshur-nirari I, 101.
Asshur-uballit, 20, 59, 61, 94, 108.
Assyrian canon, 8.
Astronomical data, 10.
Athaliah, 131 ff.
A. T. J., 84 ff.
Attalus, king of Pergamos, 187.
Augustus, 195.
Azariah (see Uzziah).
Azariah the son of Oded, 128.

BAASHA, 126 ff.
Babylon and Palestine, 41.
Babylon under Tiglath-pilezer, 147.
Babylon sacked by Sennacherib, 149.
Babylon taken by Cyrus, 161.
Babylonian dynasties, 24 ff.
Bagoses, 173, 174.
Barak, 93.
Bardes, 163.
Baruch, 157.
Bau-ahh-iddina, 135.
Bekneranef, 139.
Bel-ibni, 149.
Bel-kudur-utsur, 99.
Bel-nirari, 60, 108.
Belshazzar, 161.
Bel-shum-iddina I, 99.
Bel-shum-iddina II, 105.
Benhadad, 130 ff.
Benhadad, son of Hazael, 137.
Benjamin, civil war, 89.
Berosus, 7, 8, 183.
Bibé of Babylon, 97.
Bible chronology not superseded, 32.
Boaz, 107.
Bochim, Angel at, 87.
Breasted on Egyptian chronology, 20 ff.
Budu-ilu, 60, 94, 108.
Burna-buriash, 20, 59 ff., 108.
Byzantium founded, 151.

CALEB, 73, 75.
Cambyses, 163.
Canaanites, their extermination, 86.
Canopus inscription, 186.
Captivity, the, 156.
Carchemish, battle of, 157.
Cato the elder, 188.

Census numbers, 62, 70.
Cheronea, 182.
Chronicles, Books of, 173, 186.
Chronicon, 8.
Chronographia, 8.
Chronology: Assyrian, 8, 9, 17, 18, 134 ff.; Babylonian, 9, 17 ff., 23 ff.; 145 ff.; Biblical, data of, 5, 7; Biblical, 1st period, 35; Biblical, 2d period, 77; Biblical, 3d period, 125; Biblical, 4th period, 177; Biblical, value of, 16 ff.; Comparative, 16, 19, 23, 26, 30 ff.; Compendiums of, 7; Connecting links, 10; Egyptian, 19 ff., 26, 30 ff.; Septuagint, 7.
Cicero, 193.
Cleopatra, 187.
Cleopatra, wife of Euergetes II, 191.
Compromise chronologies, 16.
Conquest east of Jordan, 72.
Conquest by Joshua, 85.
Convocation, the great, 169.
Counting units of time, 14.
Covenant of circumcision, 37.
Covenant of the parts, 37.
Crassus, 193.
Crossing the Jordan, 72.
Ctesias, 173.
Cunaxa, battle of, 173.
Cushan-rishathaim, 75, 84, 85.
Cyrus, 161.
Cyrus the younger, 173.

DANIEL, 157.
Darius Codomannus, 182.
Darius, Hystaspis, 163.
Darius the Mede, 160.
Darius Nothus, 171.
Data as given in nature of events, 5, 6.
Data in time words, 5.
Dates of accessions, how counted, 29.
David, 80 ff., 112 ff., 117 ff.
Deborah, 93.
Demetrius Nicator, 190.
Demetrius Phalereus, 184.
Demetrius Soter, 189.
Demosthenes, 175.
Deportations by Tiglath-pilezer, 145.
Deuteronomy, 72.
Dionysius of Syracuse, 173.
Divisions of the history and the chronology, 28.
Draco at Athens, 155.

EARTHQUAKE of Uzziah, 140 ff.
Ecclesiasticus, 184, 186, 188, 190.
Eclipse of Asshur-daan, 143.
Eglon, 89.

TOPICAL INDEX

Egypt: shepherd kings, 41; 18th dynasty, 41; 20th dynasty, 73; 21st dynasty, 109 ff. See Chronology, Egyptian.
Ehud, 91.
Elah, 129.
Elam in Palestine, 41.
Eleazar the highpriest, 184.
Eli, 98, 107 ff.
Eliashib, 167.
Eliezer son of Dodavah, 132.
Elijah, 130 ff.
Elisha, 130 ff.
Elon, 105.
Epaminondas, 175.
Ephes-dammim, 115.
Epicurus, 183.
Eponym canon, 8, 134 ff.
Eras, 7, 179.
Esarhaddon, 151.
Esau, 43 ff.
Essenes, 190.
Esther, 167.
Esther, translation of, 188.
Euripides, 169.
Evil-merodach, 159.
Exodus, 71.
Explorations, 8.
Extermination of Canaanites, 86.
Ezekiel, 157.
Ezra, 167.

FAMINE, years of, 53.
Father, tribal, 42.
Foreign wives, 167.
Forty-year periods, 79, 86.

GAD the prophet, 118.
Gibeon, battle of, 72.
Gideon, 95 ff.
Gods of Babylon, fugitive, 148 ff.
Gomates, 163.
Goshen, land of, 56.
Granicus, battle of, 182.
Great Synagogue, 182.
Greek invasion, Rameses III, 80, 85.
Greek and Roman sources, 7.

HABAKKUK, 157.
Hadad, 121.
Hadrach, 142 ff.
Haggai, 163.
Hammurabi, 24, 37.
Hanani, 128.
Haremsaf, 127.
Harmhab, 61.
Hazael, 133 ff.
Heliodorus and Onias, 188.
Herod, 194.
Herodotus, 169.
Hero judges, 85, 96.
Hexateuch completed, 89.
Hezekiah, 147.
Hillel, 194.
Hippocrates, 171.
Hommel, Professor Fritz, 25.
Hosea, 141.
Hoshea, 145 ff.
Huldah, 155.
Hyrcanus, John, 190.

Hyrcanus, son of Janneas, 193.
Hyrcanus, son of Joseph, 187 ff.

IBZAN, 105.
Iddo, 126.
Ikhn-aton, 58.
Ilulaeus, 147.
Interregna, 139, 141, 145.
Interregna, Babylonian, 148.
Introduction, 5.
Introduction to 2d table, 79.
Introduction to 4th table, 179.
Isaac, 39 ff., 46.
Is-amme . . . ti, 97.
Ishbosheth, 82, 116 ff.
Ishmael, 37 ff., 42, 47, 51.
Isaiah, 143 ff.
Isiniladanus, 153.
Isocrates, 173.
Israelites in Egypt, 57; their numbers, 62.
Issachar, 49.
Issus, battle of, 182.

JABIN, 91.
Jacimus, 189.
Jacob, 43 ff., 52 ff.
Jaddua, highpriest, 175, 181.
Jadon, 126, 154.
Jahaziel, 132.
Jair, 99.
Janneas, Alexander, 191.
Janus, gate of, 186, 194, 195.
Jason, highpriest, 189.
Jedo (see Jadon).
Jehoahaz, 135.
Jehoahaz of Judah, 155.
Jehoash of Israel, 137.
Jehoiachin, 155 ff.
Jehoiada, 135.
Jehoiakim, 157.
Jehoram of Judah, 131 ff.
Jehoshaphat, 128 ff., 131 ff.
Jehu, 133 ff.
Jehu, son of Hanani, 128.
Jephthah, 102 ff.
Jeremiah, 155.
Jeroboam, 121 ff.
Jeroboam II, 137 ff.
Jerusalem destroyed by Nebuchadnezzar, 157.
Jeshua, highpriest, 161.
Jesus, birth of, 195.
Jethro, 66.
Jezebel, 129 ff.
Joab, 83.
Joash of Judah, 133.
Johanan, highpriest, 173, 181.
Joiada, highpriest, 171.
Joiakim, highpriest, 165.
Jonah, 139.
Jonathan, 112 ff.
Jonathan Maccabaeus, 189.
Joram of Israel, 133.
Jordan, crossing of, 72.
Joseph, 51 ff.
Joseph, son of Tobias, 186.
Josephus, 7, 64, 74, 80, 84, etc.
Joshua, 73 ff., 85.
Joshua: his times, 79.
Josiah, 153.

Jotham, 145.
Judas Aristobulus, 191.
Judas Maccabaeus, 189.
Jugurthine war, 191.
Julian era, 194.
Julian period, 194.
Julius Caesar, 193 ff.

KADASHMAN-BURIASH, 97.
Kadashman-hharbe, 99.
Kadashman-turgu, 60, 108.
Kadesh, 71.
Kallimmasin, 57, 108.
Kara-hhardash, 108.
Kara-indash, 108.
Kassite dynasty, 47 ff., 63 ff., 108.
Kenite and Midianite, 66.
Keturah, 41 ff.
Kudur-bel, 108.
Kuri-galzu the second, 61, 108.

LABAN, 41, 47.
Latest Old Testament events, 172.
Leah, 46 ff., 53.
Lepsius: his chronology, 20.
Livius Andronicus, 186.
Livy, 194.
Long numbers, 5, 18, 24 ff., 156, 191.

MACEDONIAN war, 187 ff.
Mahler: his chronology, 20.
Malachi, 171.
Manasseh the king, 149.
Manasseh the Samaritan, 173.
Manasseh the highpriest, 185.
Manda, the, 154, 161.
Manetho, 7 ff., 23, 186.
Marathon, 165.
Marduk-baladhsu-ikbi, 135.
Marduk-bel-usati, 133.
Marduk-nadin-ahhi, 24, 109.
Marduk-pal-iddina, 103.
Marduk-shapik-zer-mati, 109.
Mariha of Damascus, 137.
Marius, 191.
Mas, 86, 87.
Melchizedek, 37.
Meli-shihu, 101.
Menahem, 143.
Menelaus, highpriest, 189.
Mephibosheth, 82.
Merneptah, 20, 71.
Merodach-baladan, 146 ff.
Merom, waters of, 72.
Messenian war, 149.
Mesha, 132 ff.
Meyer, Edouard : his chronology, 20.
Micah the prophet, 145.
Micah (Micaiah), son of Imlah, 132.
Midian, 43, 67.
Midianite oppression, 95.
Miltiades, 165.
Moab, 39, 41; conquered by Omri, 131.
Moabite oppression, 89.
Moabite stone, 130 ff.
Moses, 65 ff., 72.
Mushezib-marduk, 149.
Mutakkil-nusku, 105.

TOPICAL INDEX

NAAMAN, 132 ff.
Nabonidus, 24, 161.
Nabopolassar, 155.
Nabu-aplu-iddina, 131.
Nabu-shum-ishkun, 127.
Nadab, 127.
Nadius, 147.
Nahum, 153.
Nathan, 118.
Nazi-bugash, 61, 108.
Nazi-murudash, 60, 108.
Nebo-dan, 101.
Nebuchadnezzar I, 104 ff.
Nebuchadnezzar, 157.
Neco of Egypt, 155.
Nehemiah, 169.
Nergal-ushezib, 149.
Neriglissar, 159.
Nineveh, downfall of, 157.
Ninip-pilezer, 99.

OBADIAH, 137.
Octavius, 194.
Oded I, 128.
Oded II, 145.
Og, 72.
Old Testament completed, 173.
Olympiads, 179.
Olynthian war, 182.
Omri, 129 ff.
Onias I, 181.
Onias II, 186.
Onias III, 189.
Onias and Heliodorus, 188.
Onias of Egypt, 189.
Oppression in Egypt, 63.
Osorkon I, 127.
Osorkon II, 133.
Osorkon III, 139.
Othniel, 87.
Ovid, 195.

PARIAN Chronicle, 185.
Parthenon, 169.
Pashé, dynasty of, 105, 111.
Pedibast, 139.
Pekah, 145.
Pekahiah, 143.
Peloponnesian war, 171.
Pemou, 139.
Pericles, 169.
Pharaoh and Moses, 70.
Pharaoh of Joseph, 52.
Pharaoh's daughter, 119.
Pharisees, 190.
Phidias, 169.
Philip of Macedonia, 175.
Philistia, Assyrian invasions, 145.
Philistine oppressions, 93, 99.
Philistines, 37 ff., 44 ff., 71, 81 ff., 93, 99, 107, 112 ff.
Philo, 195.
Phinehas, 89.
Phocion, 175.
Pindar, 165.
Pisistratus, 159.
Plataea, 167.
Plato, 173.
Polycrates, 161.
Pompey, 193.
Porus, 147.

Pseudo-smerdis, 163.
Ptolemy, canon of, 8, 18, 23, 144 ff.
Ptolemy Epiphanes, 187.
Ptolemy Euergetes I, 185 ff.
Ptolemy Euergetes II, 189 ff.
Ptolemy Lagus, 183.
Ptolemy Lathyrus, 191 ff.
Ptolemy Philadelphus, 184.
Ptolemy Philometer, 188.
Ptolemy Philopator, 187.
Pul, 142.
Punic wars, 185 ff.
Pyrrhus, 185.
Pythagoras, 161.
Pythian games, 157.

RACHEL, 46, 51.
Rameses I, 63.
Rameses II, 20, 65.
Rameses III, 75, 79, 84 ff.
Ramman-aplu-iddina, 109.
Ramman-nadin-ahhi, 95, 108.
Ramman-nirari I, 60, 94, 108.
Ramman-nirari II, 113, 126 ff.
Ramman-nirari III, 135.
Rammam-shum-iddina, 99.
Ramman-shum-utsur, 99.
Records of the Past, 32 and often.
Regillus, Lake, battle of, 165.
Rehoboam, 122 ff.
Rezin, 145.
Roman sources, 7.
Rome burnt by Gauls, 173.
Rome founded, 145.
Ruth, 107.

SADDUCEES, 190.
Salamis, 167.
Samaria founded, 131.
Samaria overthrown, 147.
Samaritans in Egypt, 184.
Samaritan schism, 172.
Samson, 99, 101.
Samuel, 106 ff., 110, 114 ff.
Sanballat, 170.
Sarah: her death, 41.
Sargon, 147.
Saul, 112 ff.
Schrader, 32.
Scythian invasion, 153.
Second Samuel, order of events, 80.
Seder olam, 7.
Seleucid era, 179, 183.
Seleucus Kallinicus, 186.
Seleucus Keraunos, 186.
Seleucus Nicator, 183.
Seleucus Philopator, 188.
Sennacherib, 24, 94, 147.
Sennacherib and gods of Babylon, 108.
Septuagint, 184.
Seti I, 63.
Shabaka of Egypt, 21, 139, 147.
Shagashalti-buriash, 89, 108.
Shagashalti-shuriash, 97.
Shalmanezer I, 91, 94, 108.
Shalmanezer II, 131 ff.
Shalmanezer III, 136.
Shalmanezer IV, 147.
Shallum, 143.
Shamash-mudammiq, 127.

Shamash-ramman, 135.
Shamash-shum-ukin, 151.
Shamgar, 93.
Shammai, 194.
Sheba, son of Bichri, 80, 120.
Sheba, Queen of, 121.
Shechem, convocation, 85.
Shemaiah, 127.
Shepherd kings, 37.
Sheshonk I (Shishak), 21 ff., 121 ff., 127.
Sheshonk III, 137, 139.
Sheshonk IV, 139.
Shiloh, 74 ff., 107.
Sicilian wars, 171.
Sihon, 72.
Simon the Just, 172, 182.
Simon II, highpriest, 187.
Simon Maccabaeus, 190.
Smith, George, 32.
Socrates, 171.
Solomon, 80 ff., 119 ff.
Solon at Athens, 157.
Sophocles, 167.
Sothic cycle, 19.
Stephen concerning Moses, 66.
Successive judges, 96.
Sulla, 191.
Synagogue, the great, 182.
Syncellus, 8.

TABLES of dates, 35 ff., 77 ff., 125 ff., 177 ff.
Tables, explanations of, 28.
Tabulation the true method, 15.
Takelot I, 129.
Takelot II, 135.
Tarquin of Rome, 163.
Taskwork, *mas.*, 86.
Temple built, 119.
Temple, David's preparations, 80 ff.
Temple, Herod's, 195.
Temple, Zerubbabel's, 161.
Tent of meeting, 71, 85.
Terence, 189.
Territory, distribution of, 72 ff., 85.
Thebes, sack of, 151.
Themistocles, 165.
Theocritus, 185.
Thermopylae, 167.
Thespis and tragedy, 161.
Thucydides, 169.
Thutmose III, 20 ff., 51.
Thutmose IV, 55.
Tiberius, 195.
Tibni, 129.
Tiglath-pilezer I, 107 ff.
Tiglath-pilezer III, 142 ff.
Tirhakah, 21, 149.
Tola, 97.
Tribute, *mas.*, 86.
Tukulti-ninip I, 25, 95, 108.
Tukulti-ninip II, 129.
Twenty years of waiting, 109 ff.
Tyre, siege of, 157.

UMMANIGAS of Elam, 147.
Uriah the Hittite, 80 ff., 116 ff.
Uriah the prophet, 157.
Ussher chronology, 16, 30 ff., 137 ff.
Uzziah, 138, 141 ff.
Uzzi-u-mash, 108.

VASHTI, 165.
Vergil, 194.

"WANDERING" in the wilderness, 73.

XENOPHON, 173.
Xerxes: See Ahasuerus.

YEAR: the ancient, 11; different kinds of, 13; Egyptian, 19 ff.; Jewish, 11; in Old Testament, 11; Olympian, 179; Roman, 179; Seleucid, 179, 183; Vernal, 11, 12.
Yukin-zer, 147.

ZAMA-SHUM-IDDINA, 103.
Zechariah, son of Iddo, 163.
Zechariah, son of Jehoiada, 137.
Zechariah, son of Jeroboam II, 143.
Zedekiah, 157.
Zephaniah, 153.
Zerah, 129.
Zimri, 129.

www.ingramcontent.com/pod-product-compliance
Lightning Source LLC
Chambersburg PA
CBHW051924160426
43198CB00012B/2030